Girls Getaway Guide
to Orlando

Girls Getaway Guide to Orlando

Leave Your Baggage at Home

Casey Wohl

Gray Dog Publishing
ORLANDO, FLORIDA

Every effort has been made to ensure that this book is as up-to-date as possible at the time of going to press. Some details, however, such as phone numbers, opening hours, prices and travel information are subject to change.

The publisher cannot accept responsibility for any consequences arising from the use of this book, nor third party websites, and cannot guarantee that any website address in this book will be a suitable source of travel information. We value the readers' views and suggestions. Please write to:
Gray Dog Publishing, PO Box 2589, Orlando, FL 32802.
www.GirlsGetawayGuide.net

First printing 2007

ISBN 978-0-9790748-3-7
LCCN 2007922052

ATTENTION CORPORATIONS, UNIVERSITIES, COLLEGES, AND PROFESSIONAL ORGANIZATIONS: Quantity discounts are available on bulk purchases of this book for educational, gift purposes, or as premiums for increasing magazine subscriptions or renewals. Special books or book excerpts can also be created to fit specific needs. For information, please contact Gray Dog Publishing, P.O. Box 2589, Orlando, FL 32802; (863) 224-6326.

www.GirlsGetawayGuide.net

TABLE OF CONTENTS

INTRODUCTION

I always used to think of Orlando as a touristy haven of theme parks and tacky T-shirts shops. That is, until I lived there for three years and realized the city had amazing shopping, superb hotels and spas, delicious restaurants, and first-class cultural events—making it an ideal location for a "Girls Getaway" trip.

I was first introduced to "Girls Getaways" by my mother, Jeri. Let me say that my mom is an original. Growing up in the 1960s, she was the typical hippie wild child. She ran away from home and went to Woodstock, hitchhiked across Florida, mingled with rock stars, and lived the wild life. Then she met my dad, got married, had three kids, and was (and still is) a terrific mother. As my brothers and I grew up and left the house, Mom formed a group of women called "The PMS Group" (or PMSers for short). This group of women gets together on a regular basis, whether at each other's homes or on getaway trips. It was because of my exposure to this group that I realized the tremendous value of the therapy that spending time with your friends can provide. My mom and her friends are a wacky and wonderful group who do not hold back on fun.

As I went through some rough times in my own life, I too turned to my girlfriends for love and support. I found these relationships and the time I spent with them was better than any professional therapy. We started having getaways in Orlando, New York, and Nashville—some of my favorite towns. I'll never forget these special trips and the huge impact the experiences with my girlfriends had on me during the good times and the bad. They accept me for who I am and whatever crazy things I may do. Great relationships with girlfriends are really like no other, and you must spend time with each other to leave your baggage behind and remember what is important. You only have one life...so make it memorable!

When my old college roommates and I began this annual trip to Orlando to revisit our alma mater Rollins College, we did not adequately research what to do, where to stay, or where to eat. We thought that just because we had lived in the city, we knew where to go. We did remember some of the old hangouts; however, the city changes very quickly, and we were not aware of some of the new places we should try.

With a few years of experience now, we have done extensive research on how to have the perfect Girls Getaway weekend in Orlando. From where to stay, where to eat, where to shop, where to get pampered, where to get cultured, and where to have fun—we have done it all!

College roommates Colleen, Sharon, and me at the Keith Urban concert during one of our Girlfriends Getaway trips to Orlando. This was one of our favorite nights.

So, for all girls who want to get away, I have compiled highlights for your Orlando travels in this convenient travel guide. From cultural and natural attractions to the trendiest new restaurants and shopping areas, this book is a must-have for any girl visiting the Orlando area.

For the latest news and help in planning your Girls Getaway to Orlando, please visit

www.GirlsGetawayGuide.net

CHAPTER 1

Why Girls Gotta Get Away

Women need time with their girlfriends—for shopping, relaxing, seeing movies or shows, indulging in desserts, and staying up late to chat about life. Quality time with girlfriends is a must.

To get away from everyday life and fully enjoy these vital girlfriends' activities, Orlando has it all. Whether you're gathering for a special life occasion or simply meeting up to enjoy some "girl time," you'll find Orlando offers plenty of fun, female-friendly things to do. Nobody renews your enthusiasm, shares your hopes and dreams, helps you celebrate life's ups and downs, or understands you better than your girlfriends. If it's not already a regularly scheduled event for you, make it a priority to take a trip with the girls to Orlando.

"You are only as strong as the cocktails you drink, the hair spray you use, and the girlfriends you have."

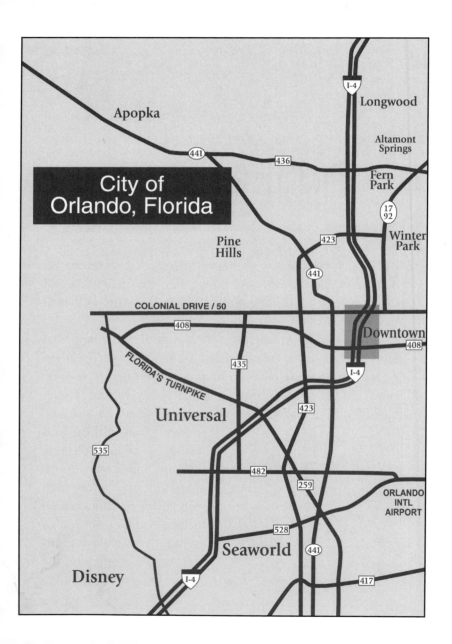

CHAPTER 2

Introduction to Orlando

P lanning your trip to Orlando should not be done at the last minute. To make the most of your visit and to avoid long waits and disappointments, take the time to make reservations and plan your days accordingly. The timing of your trip is equally as important. The off-season is typically between Thanksgiving and Christmas (an ideal shopping time for girlfriends), mid-September to mid-November, and the summer months, when the weather is hot and wet. To avoid major crowds, be sure to avoid major holidays.

Orlando stretches more than 70,000 acres and is home to more than 220,000 residents. It is the sixth largest city in Florida, the largest inland city, and home to the University of Central Florida and Rollins College. Although the city is well known for the tourist attractions in the area, such as Walt Disney World Resort, SeaWorld, and Universal Orlando Resort, there is a suprising number of cultural and natural attractions to enjoy as well. More than 52 million tourists visit Orlando each year, which is why Orlando is the second-largest city in the country for number of hotel rooms. Although Interstate 4 (also known

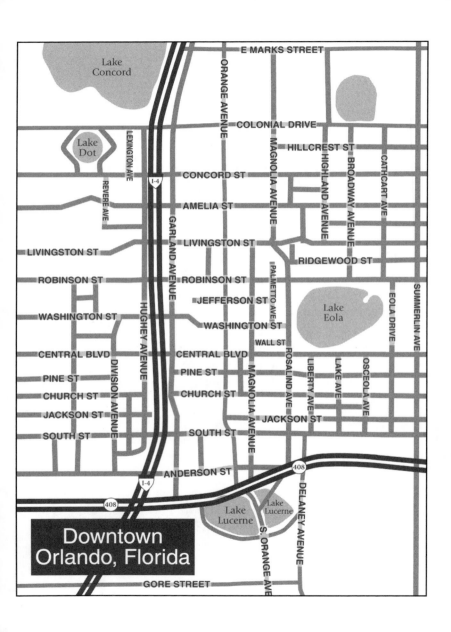

Downtown
Orlando, Florida

as I-4), the city's major highway, runs east and west in the state, it actually runs north and south through Orlando.

Orlando Areas

Disney/Lake Buena Vista: The Walt Disney World Resort is actually located in Lake Buena Vista, outside the city limits of Orlando. In addition to its four main theme parks, the resort contains two water parks, six golf courses, a sports complex, an auto race track, 20 resort hotels, and numerous shopping, dining, and entertainment offerings. The 47-square-mile property is the largest theme park resort in the world. I-4 exits include: Exits 62B (World Drive), 64B (US 192 West), 65B (Osceola Parkway West), 67B (SR 536 West), and 68 (SR 535 North). Although many people enjoy Disney, just remember that this area will be full of families particpating in the theme park experience.

Downtown Orlando: Orlando's downtown encompasses a 1,620-acre radius and is home to 17,000 residents. The main route through downtown is Orange Avenue, a one-way street on which traffic flows to the south. It is known by locals for its nightlife and for the tall office buildings. Downtown is home to many city amenities such as an 18,000-seat arena known as the TD Waterhouse Centre, which hosts sporting events, concerts, theater events, and much more. Downtown Orlando has many parks, as well as a nice outdoor eating and shopping area known as Thornton Park. Lake Eola, known for its fountain, is also a nice place to visit. Despite being away from the theme parks, downtown Orlando has recently seen much redevelopment, with many more projects currently under construction or planned. This is my recommendation for where to stay and play during a Girls Getaway in Orlando.

International Drive (I-Drive): The International Drive Resort Area is home to the nation's second largest convention center, attractions, entertainment, dining, and shopping. Here you can find unique dining experiences featuring food from just about every corner of the world. Located just off I-4, I-Drive is located north of Disney and south of downtown. With the Convention Center as the hub of I-Drive activities, the crowd in this area tends to be business-oriented but with some tourists from the theme parks as well.

Universal Orlando: The Universal area of Orlando consists of two theme parks (Universal Studios Florida and Islands of Adventure), CityWalk (a nighttime entertainment destination), and three Loews hotels. Recent ad campaigns have portrayed the park as a "grown-up" or more mature version of its Disney rival, but this is still a popular place for families to stay and enjoy the theme parks. Universal Orlando is located north of the International Drive resort area, on a parcel of land framed by I-4 to the south, State Road 435/Kirkman Road to the east, Vineland Road to the north, and Turkey Lake Road to the west. The resort is directly accessible from I-4 via Exit 74B.

Winter Park: Winter Park is a city of about 25,000 residents, located just minutes north of Orlando. It is famous for its bricked streets, lakes, beautiful parks, unique shops, Rollins College, the Winter Park Farmer's Market, and impressive art festivals. The 11-acre Central Park is bordered by Park Avenue, which boasts excellent boutique shopping, delicious cuisine, and fabulous museums and art galleries. Often referred to as the "Palm Beach" of Orlando, the Winter Park atmosphere is quaint with terrific shopping and great culture.

CHAPTER 3

Where to Stay

Included in this chapter are some recommended hotels broken down by where in Orlando they are located. The closer you are to a theme park, the more families you will find in the nearby hotels. If you are looking for a kid-free weekend, I recommend staying downtown or in Winter Park. Along International Drive, near the Orange County Convention Center, you will find more business travelers or people attending a convention. Price categories for a one-night stay in a standard room without taxes are as follows:

$$$$$	$400+
$$$$	$300–400
$$$	$200–300
$$	$100–200
$	< $100

Disney/Lake Buena Vista

Omni Orlando Resort at ChampionsGate—$$–$$$$$

1500 Masters Boulevard, ChampionsGate, FL 33896;
407-390-6664; www.championsgate.com

Golfers and non-golfers alike enjoy the ChampionsGate 15-acre recreation area, which includes an 850-foot lazy river, two heated pools with private cabanas surrounded by towering palms and fountains, and a lighted nine-hole, par-three golf course. Girl-friends can also relax at a European-style spa with indoor and outdoor treatments rooms, work out at a full-service health club, and dine at one of five onsite restaurants.

Located just minutes from the major Disney theme parks, ChampionsGate activities also include one 9-hole and two 18-hole golf courses designed by Greg Norman, plus a nearby golf academy for girls who need to brush up on their strokes.

Gaylord Palms Resort & Convention Center—$$$–$$$$

6000 W. Osceola Parkway, Kissimmee, FL 34746;
407-586-0000; www.gaylordhotels.com

With its signature glass atrium, the Gaylord Palms Resort & Convention Center features more than four acres of resort living. Set in the style and grandeur of a turn-of-the-century Florida mansion, the hotel features natural-themed Florida living, from historic St. Augustine to festive Key West to the everglades. Amenities include the Canyon Ranch SpaClub, South Beach swimming pool with cabanas, shopping, live nightly entertainment, and three restaurants and lounges, including Auggie's Jammin' Piano Bar.

Grand Floridian Resort—$$$$$

4401 Grand Floridian Way, Lake Buena Vista, FL 32830;
407-824-2421; www.disneyworld.com

Known as Disney's flagship hotel, the Grand Floridian is a luxu-
rious Victorian-themed resort. Amenities include a pool, white
sand beach, monorail service to the Disney parks, exceptional
dining, and a full-service spa. Dining options include the exclusive Victoria & Albert's.

Hyatt Regency Grand Cypress—$$$$

One Grand Cypress Boulevard, Orlando, FL 32836;
407-238-1234; www.hyattgrandcypress.com

This four-diamond, 1,500-acre resort boasts some outstanding
guest amenities for girls in need of "getting away from it all." A
beach, extravagant pool, equestrian center, tennis facilities, golf
course, and spa will keep you busy. A white-sand beach and
marina are highlights on the hotel's 21-acre Lake Windsong,
where guests can enjoy sailboats, paddleboats, and canoes. The
pool covers more than a half-acre as it flows through grottos
and caves, past a dozen waterfalls and a 45-foot slide. For adventurous guests, pleasure rides or English-riding lessons are
available at the 10-acre equestrian center. Tennis fans can visit
the Grand Cypress Racquet Club, which offers clinics, lessons,
and twelve tennis courts half lighted for evening play. Golfers
can frequent the 45 holes of Jack Nicklaus Signature Design, a
nine-hole putt-putt course and a first-class golf academy.

Downtown Orlando

Courtyard by Marriott Orlando Downtown—$$

730 North Magnolia Avenue, Orlando, FL 32803;
407-996-1000

Relax and enjoy the comforts of home at the Courtyard. Reasonably priced with a great downtown location, this hotel is close to great restaurants, museums, sports centers, and event venues. Amenities include a heated outdoor pool, Jacuzzi, and fitness center.

Eō Inn & Urban Spa—$$

227 North Eola Drive, Orlando, FL 32801;
407-481-8485; www.eoinn.com

Overlooking the downtown skyline in Thornton Park, the Eō Inn & Urban Spa is a boutique hotel located on Lake Eola. The elegant yet understated interiors feature many personal touches. Enjoy relaxing lakeside walks with all the downtown activities just minutes away. Complimentary breakfast included.

The Courtyard at Lake Lucerne—$$

211 North Lucerne Circle, Orlando, FL 32801;
407-648-5188; www.orlandohistoricinn.com

This award-winning, historic bed and breakfast is tucked away in an intimate garden setting in downtown Orlando. It's within walking distance of Orlando's business district and a short drive to the theme parks. The Courtyard offers an eclectic collection of accommodations within its four historic buildings ranging in style from Victorian, antebellum, and art-deco to Grand Victorian.

Orlando Downtown Marriott—$$–$$$

400 West Livingston Street, Orlando, FL 32801;
407-843-6664; www.marriott.com

Located in the heart of Orlando, the Marriott is conveniently located directly across from the Bob Carr Performing Arts Centre and the TD Waterhouse Arena—great for avoiding parking at these venues, but challenging if you plan to arrive at or depart from the hotel during these events. Amenities include a 24-hour fitness center and cardio theater, heated pool and Jacuzzi, sports bar, and steak and seafood restaurant and café.

The Veranda Bed & Breakfast—$$

115 North Summerlin Avenue, Orlando, FL 32801;
407-849-0321; www.theverandabandb

This European-style bed and breakfast is located in historic Thornton Park, which is home to great eateries and trendy shops, as well as a short walk to Lake Eola and downtown Orlando. The Veranda features a garden courtyard and five historic buildings dating back to the early 1900s.

Westin Grand Bohemian—$$–$$$

325 South Orange Avenue, Orlando, FL 32801;
407-313-9000; www.grandbohemianhotel.com

My favorite hotel in downtown Orlando, the Westin Grand Bohemian reigns as the city's landmark luxury hotel. Not only is the hotel gorgeous and comfortable, but it also features a great location in downtown Orlando, serves as an art gallery, and features live music in the Klimt Rotunda, an outdoor heated pool, in-room or poolside massage treatments, award-winning cuisine, heavenly bed and bath accessories, the Boheme Restaurant, the Bösendorfer Lounge (named "Best Place to Sip Martinis" by the *Orlando Business Journal*), a fabulous Sunday jazz brunch, and a Starbucks right in the lobby. The hotel is close to galleries, boutiques, cafés, and exciting nightspots. Plus, guests on the 15th floor enjoy upgraded amenities including a Bose CD Wave stereo radio and access to the exclusive lounge, serving complimentary continental breakfast and evening hors d'oeuvres, with available cash bar service. Highly recommended.

International Drive

Baymont Inn & Suites Convention Center I-Drive—$

8342 Jamaican Court, Orlando, FL 32819;
407-363-1944; www.baymontinns.com

Hospitality at down-to-earth prices, the Baymont is located just off I-Drive and minutes from attractions. It also offers free continental breakfast, local calls, high-speed Internet, coffee/tea, a heated pool, and cable TV, and is close to the Orange County Convention Center.

La Quinta Inn at International Drive—$

8300 Jamaican Court, Orlando, FL 32819;
407-351-1660; 800-332-1660; www.lq.com

Located just off I-Drive and a half-mile from the convention center, the La Quinta offers standard, deluxe, and king rooms, complimentary deluxe continental breakfast bar, heated pool, spa, and the Barefoot Bar. Free Disney shuttle and high speed Internet. Pets welcome.

Peabody Orlando—$$$–$$$$$

9801 International Drive, Orlando, FL 32819;
407-352-4000; 800-732-2639; www.peabodyorlando.com

Here, you'll find marching ducks...yes, live marching ducks! The Peabody is an 891-room luxury hotel, best known for the daily march of ducks that descend via elevator from their penthouse down to the hotel lobby, a must-see event for Peabody guests. Located directly across from the convention center and close to shopping, theme parks, and performing and visual arts, this hotel offers luxury and convenience. The property is also home to an athletic club, a heated full-size lap/swimming pool with a pool bar and cabanas, a spa and salon, sauna and tennis. Hotel dining options include Capriccio Bar & Grill, an Italian steakhouse; Dux, providing first-class dining; and Peabody Wine Cellar.

The Ritz-Carlton Grande Lakes— $$$–$$$$$

4012 Central Florida Parkway, Orlando, FL 32837;
407-206-2400; www.ritzcarlton.com

Although not on I-Drive, the Ritz is only about 3.5 miles away. This 500-acre property is surrounded by lush tropical gardens, lakes, and the headwaters to the Florida everglades. All rooms feature hand-painted Italian furniture and a private balcony with views of the lakes, gardens, and pool. The resort offers a wide selection of packages, including shopping trips, spa visits, and special golf rates. A favorite, the "Reconnect" package, starts at $219 per night and includes deluxe room accommodations, breakfast buffet for two, and a $25–$50 spa or golf credit. Activities at the resort include the Ritz-Carlton Spa, a Greg

Norman-designed 18-hole golf course, three lighted tennis courts, Orvis–endorsed fly-fishing school, Eco-Tours on Shingle Creek, bicycle rental, a jogging trail, and a lazy river pool.

Universal Orlando

Hard Rock Hotel—$$$–$$$$$

5800 Universal Boulevard, Orlando, FL 32819;
407-503-2000; www.hardrock.com

Have you always wanted to live like a rock star? Now you can at Orlando's 650-room Hard Rock Hotel at the Universal Orlando Resort. Rock star features include $1 million worth of authentic rock 'n' roll memorabilia throughout the hotel, a 12,000-square foot swimming pool with a sand beach and underwater music, private music-themed poolside cabanas, impeccable accommodations (including 29 suites, Club Level rooms on the 7th floor, and the 2,000-square-foot Graceland Suite), and complimentary water taxi or shuttle to the Universal CityWalk entertainment complex and both Universal Orlando theme parks. The resort also offers pet-friendly rooms. Although you don't have to be a rock star to stay here, you will certainly grow accustomed to the lifestyle. Restaurants and bars include the Palm, the Kitchen, Velvet, and Beachclub.

Orlando Portofino Bay Hotel—$$$–$$$$$

5601 Universal Boulevard, Orlando, FL 32819;
407-503-1000; www.loewshotels.com

The hotel is a stunning re-creation of the famed Mediterranean seaside resort village of Portofino, Italy. You'll feel like you arrived at the Mediterranean while visiting this award-winning hotel. Located within walking distance of the Universal theme parks and the Universal CityWalk, guest transportation is available. Recreation includes three themed swimming pools, scenic jogging paths, bocce ball courts, and the full-service Mandara Spa. Guests can also enjoy hotel activities from live music to cooking demonstrations to wine tastings. Restaurants and lounges include Bice Ristorante, Mama Della's Ristorante, Trattoria Del Porto, and Bar American.

Winter Park

La Quinta Orlando/Winter Park—$–$$

626 Lee Road, Orlando, FL 32810;
407-645-5600 ; 877-807-8777; www.lqinn.com

Featuring 200 newly-renovated rooms and free breakfast, the La Quinta is perfect for girls on a budget who still want to enjoy the Winter Park atmosphere.

The Park Plaza Hotel—$$–$$$

307 Park Avenue South, Winter Park, FL 32789;
407-647-1072; www.parkplazahotel.com

Built in 1922 and located on Park Avenue, the Park Plaza Hotel is classic sophistication in a small, intimate hotel. In keeping with these early traditions of personal service and hospitality, the Park Plaza's renovations have preserved this hotel's quiet elegance. A balcony garden with ferns, potted plants, and brilliantly colored flowers overlooks Park Avenue. We always enjoy a glass of wine on the balcony while watching the Park Avenue happenings. A complimentary continental breakfast or evening cocktails can be enjoyed in this old-fashioned setting. Guests may enjoy room service or dine at the hotel's award-winning Park Plaza Gardens restaurant.

CHAPTER 4

Where to Shop

What kind of girlfriends' getaway would it be without shopping? With nine malls, several outlet centers, and dozens of neighborhood shopping centers and boutiques, you'll have no problem finding a shopping area all the girls will enjoy exploring.

Malls

Fashion Square Mall

3201 East Colonial Drive (Highway 50), Orlando, FL 32803; 407-896-1131; www.orlandofashionsquare.com

Anchored by Dillard's, Macy's, Sears, and JC Penney, this mall just east of downtown features stores such as American Eagle Outfitters, Ann Taylor Loft, Bath & Body Works, Body Shop, Bombay Company, Charlotte Russe, Express, the

> *"I base most of my fashion taste on what doesn't itch."*
>
> —GILDA RADNER

Limited, Nine West, Things Remembered, Victoria's Secret, and White Barn Candle. Dining options include Charley's Grilled Subs, Chik-Fil-A, Manchu Wok, Panera Bread, Pita & More, Quizno's Subs, Rudy Tuesday's, and Sbarros. The mall also houses the Premiere 14 Cinema.

Festival Bay Mall at International Drive

5250 International Drive, Orlando, FL 32819;
800-481-1944; www.shopfestivalbaymall.com

Hours: Monday–Saturday 10 A.M.–9 P.M., Sunday 11 A.M.–7 P.M.

Festival Bay Mall at I-Drive features more than 55 specialty stores, 11 dining destinations, and 4 exciting entertainment venues. Specialty stores include Bass Pro Shops Outdoor World, Ron Jon Surf Shop, Sheplers Western Wear, Steve and Barry's University Sportswear, Hilo Hattie—The Store of Hawaii, PacSun, Journey's, Hot Topic, Urban Planet, V Generation, and BCBG MaxAzria, plus many more. The mall also offers shoppers fun entertainment opportunities, including indoor glow-in-the-dark miniature golf at Putting Edge and Cinemark 20 Movie Theatres.

The Florida Mall

8001 South Orange Blossom Trail, Orlando, FL 32809;
407-851-6255; www.simon.com/mall

Located on the corner of S. Orange Blossom Trail (17/92/441 and Sand Lake Road)
Hours: Monday–Saturday 10 A.M.–9 P.M., Sunday noon–6 P.M.

The area's largest mall with more than 250 shops, including department stores Nordstrom, Macy's, Saks Fifth Avenue, and

Dillard's. With a complete renovation and expansion completed in November 1999, Florida Mall boasts more than 50 new specialty retailers, with more than 25 of those stores making their Central Florida debut. Also featured is the Thomas Kinkade Florida Mall Gallery. Restaurant highlights include Bucca Di Beppo, Le Jardin Restaurant, California Pizza Kitchen, Nordstrom Café, Salsa Taqueria & Tequila Bar, plus 15 other eateries.

The Mall at Millenia
4200 Conroy Road, Orlando, FL 32839;
www.mallatmillenia.com

From I-4, Exit #78
Hours: Monday–Saturday 10 A.M.–9 P.M., Sunday noon–7 P.M.

The Mall at Millenia is Orlando's newest mall, with more than 100 stores including department stores Macy's, Bloomingdale's, and Neiman Marcus as well as high-end retailers Burberry, Chanel, Christian Dior, Coach, Gucci, Tiffany & Company, and more, crafting a mix of international designer stores with U.S. favorites. Restaurant highlights include Brio Tuscan Grille, the Cheesecake Factory, McCormick & Schmick's Seafood Restaurant, P. F. Chang's China Bistro, California Pizza Kitchen, Panera Bread, and more. The mall also hosts the Blue Martini and the ultra-chic entertainment lounge, open seven nights a week until 2 A.M., featuring live entertainment nightly and indoor/outdoor seating.

Outdoor Shopping

Designer Row

Orange Avenue, Winter Park, FL 32789

Up and down Orange Avenue between downtown and Winter Park, you will find stores and boutiques that have served the Central Florida interior design and building community for years. These area businesses specialize in custom kitchen and bath designs, galleries, fashionable interior design, exotic tile and stone stores, art framing shops, as well as vintage clothing and jewelry.

Ivanhoe Row

1211–2010 North Orange Avenue (at Virginia Drive), Orlando, FL 32804

Located between downtown and Winter Park, Ivanhoe Row is across from Lake Formosa, which makes for beautiful park and lake setting. Here you can find several blocks of both large and quaint antique shops, with styles ranging from Victorian to art-deco to Chippendale to Asian to country classics. Find 19th- and 20th-century furniture at Swanson's Antiques; Flo's Attic is a bright pink can't-miss building housing restored furniture and estate jewelry; Pieces of Eight Antique Emporium has nearly a dozen dealers offering a wide selection of antiques; Rock N Roll Heaven offers vinyl (yes, vinyl) records; the Fredlund Wildlife Gallery has a selection of paintings and sculptures of your favorite wild-life; the Fly Fisherman is a fly-fishing haven with all the equipment needed; the William Moseley Gallery has 19th-century oil paintings; and Tim's Wine Market is a popular wine store offering hundreds of labels. There are also upscale women's and men's fashions, as well as vintage clothing stores.

Park Avenue Shops
Located along Park Avenue, north of Fairbanks Avenue

Escape the hustle and bustle of city life by spending a peaceful day in the scenic Park Avenue Winter Park shopping district. The main street in Winter Park, Park Avenue is lined with al fresco cafés, upscale boutiques and gift shops, home decor galleries and museums, posh clothing stores, and unique stationery shops. Across from the shopping is Central Park, a beautifully manicured green space complete with large, shady oak trees. On Park Avenue you'll find Jacobson's, Williams-Sonoma, the Gap, Ann Taylor, Pottery Barn, Lucky Brand Jeans, Storehouse, Nicole Miller, Peterbrooke Chocolatier, Restoration Hardware, Williams-Sonoma, Lily Pulitzer, Downeast Orvis, and Talbot's. Unique boutiques include the Doggie Door for all your pet needs; Tuni's, a trendy women's clothing store featuring designer labels; Shou'ture, where you can shop for the hippest shoes and get a pedicure; Vino!, for all of your wine needs; and Partridge Tree and Red Marq, a favorite of mine for unique stationery, cards, and gifts. Other shops include Bliss On Park Avenue and the Paper Shop. Dining options span the globe, ranging from Pannullos Italian Restaurant to Café De France to the Turkish restaurant Bosphorous to the all-American Briarpatch. Thursdays on Park Avenue (6–9 P.M.) include extended hours at most stores and galleries, live music, discount meals at select restaurants, and free valet parking.

Winter Park Village

460 North Orlando Avenue, Winter Park, FL 32789;
407-644-0129; www.shopwinterparkvillage.com

A quaint outdoor shopping area, the Winter Park Village features fine shopping in stores such as Ann Taylor Loft, Pier 1 Imports, Liz Claiborne, Jos A Bank Clothiers, Borders Books, McKenzies Hallmarka, and Russell Alexander Gallery. For entertainment, the village is home to Regal Cinemas 20 Movie Theater. Dining options are plentiful as well, with the Cheesecake Factory, P. F. Changs Chinese Bistro, Beluga Seafood & Martini Bar, Crispers Fresh Salads & Such, Ruth's Chris Steakhouse, Brio Tuscan Grille, Seito Sushi, and Marble Slab Creamery.

Pointe*Orlando

9101 International Drive,
Orlando, FL 32819;
407-248-2838;
www.pointeorlandofl.com

> *"With clothes the new are the best, with friends the old are the best."*

Easily recognizable on I-Drive by the upside down building titled "Wonderworks," Pointe*Orlando is an open-air shopping, dining, and entertainment complex, featuring more than 60 retailers, seven restaurants, and entertainment. Stores include AIX Armani Exchange, Bath & Body Works, B. Dalton Booksellers, Bimini Shoes, Boardwalk Surf Shop, Chico's, Denim Place, Everything But Water, Express, Foot Locker, Sunglass Hut, Victoria's Secret, Yankee Candle, and much more. Eateries include Adobe Gila's (margarita bar and cantina), the Capital Grill, and Starbucks.

Outlets

Lake Buena Vista Factory Stores

State Road 535, Orlando, FL 32821;
407-238-9301; www.lbvfs.com

From I-4, Exit #68

Hours: Monday–Saturday 10 A.M.–9 P.M., Sunday 10 A.M.–6 P.M.

Bargain hunters will enjoy discounts at stores such as Border's Book Outlet, Dressbarn, Eddie Bauer, Fossil, Gap, Jockey, Kitchen Collection, Liz Claiborne, London Fog, Nike, Nine West, Old Navy, Reebok, Rockport, Samsonite, Sony, Waterford Wedgewood, and much more. Be sure to ask your hotel if shuttle transportation is provided to these factory stores.

Orlando Premium Outlets

8200 Vineland Avenue, Orlando, FL 32821;
407-238-7787

From I-4, Exit #68

Hours: Monday–Saturday 10 A.M.–10 P.M., Sunday 10 A.M.–9 P.M.

Orlando's upscale outlets shopping experience with more than 110 outlet stores including Banana Republic, Barneys New York, BCBG Max Azria, Bebe, Burberry, Calvin Klein, Coach, Dior, Fendi, Giorgio Armani, Guess?, Kenneth Cole, Lacoste, Lucky Brand Blue Jeans, MaxMara, Nike, Polo Ralph Lauren, Theory, Versace, and much more.

Prime Outlets Orlando

5401 West Oak Ridge Road, Orlando, FL 32819;
407-352-9600; www.primeoutlets.com

From I-4, Exit #75A

Hours: Monday–Saturday 10 A.M.–9 P.M., Sunday 10 A.M.–7 P.M.

With more than 170 brand names, bargain hunters will enjoy Central Florida's largest outlet center. Outlet stores include Ann Taylor, Calvin Klein, COACH, Cole Haan, DKNY Jeans, Escada, Fossil, Gap, Geoffrey Beane, Guess?, Hard Rock, Harry & David, IZOD, Liz Claiborne, Nine West, Off 5th Saks Fifth Avenue, Polo Ralph Lauren, Tommy Hilfiger, and Waterford Wedgewood. The outlet is located at the north end of I-Drive and minutes from Universal Studios and Wet & Wild, and is undergoing significant improvements that will be completed in July 2007. Ask your hotel about shopping packages.

This and That

Liquidation Station, Inc.

349 North Orlando Avenue, Winter Park, FL 32789;
407-599-0067

Bargains for millionaires? Well, not exactly. This place has really cool stuff at reasonable prices. From antique reproductions of indoor and outdoor furniture, mirrors, artwork, garden statues, and more. My mother introduced me to it. I have taken several of my friends here, and everyone has a good time looking around. If nothing else, get a free bag of popcorn and peruse the unusual and often fun items found here.

Orlando Vintage Clothing Company

2117 West Fairbanks Avenue, Winter Park, FL 32789;
407-599-7225

Hours: Monday–Friday 11 A.M.–6 P.M., Saturday 10 A.M.–6 P.M.

Looking for some rare finds for dressing up or your next party costume? Look no further than this fun vintage store. Around Halloween the pickins are slim, so be sure to plan your October costume needs early.

Thornton Threads

819 East Washington Street, Orlando, FL 32801;
407-423-9922

Located downtown in Thornton Park, this is a great specialty store with a good mix of name brands, local designers, and unknown brands. Trendy clothing with somewhat of a unique vintage feel at reasonable prices.

Tim's Wine Market

1223 North Orange Avenue, Orlando, FL 32804;
407-895-9463

Hours: Monday–Thursday 10 A.M.–6 P.M., Friday 10 A.M.–7 P.M., Saturday 10 A.M.–6 P.M.

A popular wine store with Orlando locals, Tim's is one of the few wine retailers in the United States actually to conduct wine classes. Classes are popular, so be sure to call ahead for reservations.

Zou Zou Boutique

2 North Summerlin Avenue, Orlando, FL 32801;
407-843-3373; www.zouzouboutique.com

Located downtown in Thornton Park, Zou Zou is perfect for girls looking for unique clothing in an intimate setting. This is a great boutique with a wonderful selection.

CHAPTER 5

Where to Eat

With more than 5,000 restaurants in the Orlando area, you are sure to find exactly what you want. Highlighted in this chapter are some favorites in all parts of town, at all price ranges, and with various types of cuisine.

Attire:

> C = Casual
> D = Dressy

Price for dinner for two:

> $ = Less than $40
> $$ = $40–$60
> $$$ = $60–$80
> $$$$ = More than $80

Reservations:

> R = Required
> S = Suggested
> NR = Not Required

Disney/Lake Buena Vista

House of Blues

Downtown Disney
1490 East Buena Vista Drive, Lake Buena Vista, FL 32830;
407-934-BLUE; www.hob.com

Cajun/Southern; C; $$; NR; lunch, dinner

Jambalaya, po-boys, fried shrimp, cheddar cheese grits, and cornbread are some of the traditional Cajun favorites featured at this well-known chain. Decorated in quintessential New Orleans style, the HOB is best known for its live music. The Orlando HOB hosts musical acts from all genres, so be sure to visit their website for acts performing during your trip. A favorite is the gospel brunch featuring live music and all-you-can-eat Southern food.

Victoria & Albert's (disneyworld.disney.go.com/wdw/dining)

Grand Floridian Resort & Spa
4401 Grand Floridian Way, Lake Buena Vista, FL 32830;
407-939-3463; disneyworld.disney.go.com/wdw/dining

American regional; D; $$$$; R; dinner only

With a menu that changes daily, exceptional food, and impeccable service, this is the most expensive restaurant at any Disney World resort and after dining here, you'll agree it is worth it. I have not personally eaten here, but friends have and give it rave reviews.

Wolfgang Puck Grand Café

Downtown Disney
1482 East Buena Vista Drive, Lake Buena Vista, FL 32830;
407-938-9653; www.wolfgangpuck.com

American; C; $$–$$$; NR; lunch, dinner

Featuring the signature Wolfgang Puck pizza, homemade soups, a variety of salads, and a casual atmosphere, the Wolfgang Puck Grand Café offers fine cuisine for everyone. Don't overlook the desserts; the crème brulee sampler offers three flavors: vanilla bean, dark chocolate, butterscotch. In addition, the café features an excellent and affordable wine list.

Downtown Orlando

Boheme Restaurant

325 South Orange Avenue, Orlando, FL 32801;
407-313-9000; www.grandbohemianhotel.com/dining

American; D; $$$-$$$$; R; breakfast, lunch, dinner

Voted best hotel restaurant by *Orlando* magazine, the Boheme boasts eclectic cuisine featuring classic dishes with a modern twist. Appetizers include the Fricassee of Escargot, Jumbo "Peeky Toe" Crab Cake, Seared Bohemian Foie Gras or Tartare of Ahi Tuna. Soup and salad options are also unique, including Cognac Lobster Bisque, Boheme Organic Field Greens, and Hearts of Iceberg Lettuce

"Friends are the most important ingredient in this recipe of life."

with Applewood Smoked Bacon. Featured entrées range from Roasted Rack of New Zealand Lamb to Herb Smoked Pork Loin Chop to Skillet Roasted Chilean Sea Bass to Tempura Tuna Roll to Asparagus Crusted Diver Scallops. Dessert lovers will not be disappointed with options like Crème Brulee Five Ways, White Chocolate Raspberry Tower, or the very "Bohemian" trio of hand-made sorbets. You'll find plenty of reasonable wine choices, but wine connoisseurs will applaud a few well-known French and Italian bottles. Live music is featured most evenings.

Breakfast Club

63 Pine Street, Orlando, FL 32801; 407-843-1559

American; C; $; breakfast, lunch

This rare "greasy spoon" breakfast and lunch diner and coffeehouse in downtown Orlando offers breakfast during all hours of operation.

Harvey's Bistro

390 North Orange Ave., Orlando, FL 32801;
407-246-6560; www.harveybistro.com

American Cuisine; D; $$$; S; lunch (Monday–Friday), dinner, closed Sundays

This trendy, casual downtown bistro is well known for its weekday power lunches. Come in to feast on fabulous American favorites and great wines. A great location to visit before evening events in downtown Orlando.

HUE

629 East Central Boulevard, Orlando, FL 32801;
407-849-1800; www.huerestaurant.com

American Cuisine; C; $$$; S; Lunch, dinner

This critically acclaimed urban bistro provides an ultra-chic atmosphere and terrific food in downtown Orlando. HUE offers a full bar, one of downtown's hottest happy hours (be sure to check out third Thursdays of the month), and a disco brunch on the third Sunday of each month. It provides a "big city" dining experience in the heart of Orlando; I have a great meal every time I'm there.

Heather and me enjoying a fantastic meal at HUE before a concert.

Kres Chophouse & Lounge

17 West Church Street, Orlando, FL 32801;
407-447-7950; www.kresrestuarant.com

American; D; $$$; S; Lunch (Monday–Friday); dinner; closed Sundays

A classic downtown steakhouse and lounge located on historic Church Street. Kres was voted best late night dinner by *Orlando* magazine. This American chophouse has a Mediterranean influence infused in its menu, which changes daily. With a fabulous wine list and a great atmosphere, you will not be disappointed by your dining experience.

Market Street Cafe

407 East Central Boulevard, Orlando, FL 32801;
407-770-2030

American; C; $$; NR; breakfast, lunch, dinner

Boasting a fabulous view of downtown Orlando's Lake Eola, as well as delicious American "comfort" food choices, this café serves breakfast all day. The menu features traditional entrées such as eggs, pancakes, sandwiches, and burgers. The café is limited on its liquor selections and is best frequented for breakfast or lunch.

Manuel's on the 28th

390 North Orange Avenue, Orlando, FL 32801;
407-246-6580; www.manuelsonthe28th.com

Contemporary; D; $$$$; R; dinner only; closed Sundays and Mondays

Located at the top of downtown Orlando's Bank of America Building, Manuel's offers guests a lovely view of the city via ceiling-to-floor glass windows. The menu is contemporary world cuisine that changes seasonally and features nightly creations of exotic game and seafood. The wine list includes a selection of California's finest by glass and bottle as well as a captain's list of international selections.

Napasorn Thai Restaurant

56 E. Pine Street, Orlando, FL 32801;
407-245-8088; www.napasornthai.com

Thai; C; $$; S; lunch weekdays; dinner everyday

With its authentic Thai food interspersed with Chinese offerings, Napasorn is a must-stop if you like Thai food. It offers sushi in addition to lunch and dinner menus and has a wonderful dessert menu (friend ice cream). In addition, it offers domestic and imported beer, plum wine, sake, and a nice wine list. An excellent choice for anyone seeking good Thai food.

Numero Uno

2499 South Orange Avenue, Orlando, FL 32806;
407-841-3840; www.numerounorestaurant.com

Cuban; C; $–$$; NR; lunch, dinner; closed Sundays

This restaurant offers authentic, home-style Cuban food in a comfortable, casual, and festive atmosphere. Classic Cuban meals include lechón asado, the ropa vieja, and the picadillo. The arroz con pollo, a generous serving of chicken chunks in seasoned yellow rice, is wonderful.

Sam Snead's Tavern

301 East Pine Street, Orlando, FL 32801;
407-999-0109; www.samsneadstavern.com

American; C; $$–$$$; S; lunch, dinner

Across from Lake Eola and decorated with rich wood and golf memorabilia, this tavern-like restaurant attracts business types during lunch and dinner on weekdays. It is a great place for a group of people with lots of socializing and large celebratory parties. Menu selections range from salads to burgers to sandwiches to steaks to fresh fish. A new item added recently is the daily Hawaiian fish selection. Caught and shipped the day before, the fresh fish, found only in Hawaii, gives customers a rare opportunity to enjoy a variety of well-prepared meals. The desserts are also delicious. The Chocolate Sack serves four, and the Chocolate Corruption Cake is decadent.

White Wolf Café

1829 North Orange Avenue, Orlando, FL 32804;
407-895-9911; www.whitewolfcafe.com

American; C; $$: S; lunch, dinner; closed Sundays

Opened in 1991 and named after the owners' white German Shepherd, this American bistro and antique shop is conveniently located between downtown and Winter Park among a collection of antique shops referred to as Invanhoe Row. Serving soups, salads, sandwiches, entrées, foccacias, and flatbreads, the café will have something for everyone. I enjoy the salads, and favorites include the White Wolf Waldorf, the Zesty Cool Shrimp & Avocado, the Gailileo, and the Hearts of the Mediterranean.

International Drive

Bahama Breeze

8849 International Drive, Orlando, FL 32819; 407-248-2499
8735 Vineland Avenue, Orlando, FL 32821; 407-938-9010
6621 South Orange Avenue, Orlando, FL 32809; 407-251-4677
www.bahamabreeze.com

Caribbean; C; $$; NR; lunch, dinner

The three area locations of Bahama Breeze offer patio seating and live island music, along with tasty Caribbean-inspired dishes that will truly put you in vacation mode. This very cool and funky, lunch- and dinner-only restaurant serves island foods such as ropa vieja, ceviche, jerk pork, and Jamaican-grilled chicken.

Bergamos

Mercado Shopping Village
8445 International Drive, Orlando, FL 32819;
407-352-3805; www.bergamos.com

Italian; C; $$–$$$; S; dinner only

One of my mom's favorite restaurants, Bergamos offers great Italian food and wonderful live entertainment. If you enjoy musicals, this is the place for you. The wait staff frequently breaks into your favorite Broadway, Grand Opera, and Neapolitan folk tunes. I enjoy the Tagliatelle Bolognese, which is spaghetti with pieces of steak. There is also a wonderful wine list, and the restaurant is able to accommodate large groups. Try not to sit too close to the piano as it is rather loud. Although the music is excellent, your conversation will be interrupted when the singing takes place.

Bonefish Grill

7830 West Sand Lake Road, Orlando, FL 32819;
407-355-7707; www.bonefishgrill.com

American; C; $$; R; dinner

Although I am not a huge seafood fan, I love the seafood at Bonefish Grill. The fish is always fresh with unique, tasty sauces. I always order the Bang Bang Shrimp (which I could eat every day) as an appetizer. My favorite side dish is the Island Rice, and my favorite entrée is the Grouper Piccata. Honestly, all the food is great here; you cannot go wrong. There are also fantastic drinks; favorites include the Cantaloupe Martini and the Icicle Aphrodisiac.

Café Tu Tu Tango

8625 International Dr, Orlando, FL 32819;
407-248-2222; www.cafetututango.com

Multiethnic; C; $$; S; lunch, dinner

The funky décor is that of a Spanish artist's loft, making Café Tu Tu Tango an ideal spot for a group of girlfriends to dine. You don't just come here to eat, but to savor life, friends, and family. Its *tapas*-sized portions are meant to be passed around the table, with each diner ordering a favorite or two to share. All types of artists complete their masterpieces as you dine, and live music makes the mood lively and fun. Other entertainment may include belly dancing or fire or sword eaters. The first time I came here, there was a man dancing on the tables wearing a pink tutu and not much else. You never know what you will find here. With a festive atmosphere and great food, this is one of our favorite restaurants.

First Watch

7500 Sand Lake Road, Orlando, FL 32819;
407-363-5622; www.firstwatch.com

American; C; $; NR; breakfast, lunch

A diner-like breakfast, brunch, and lunch experience makes this a popular place to get both traditional and unique meals. Choices include the Key West Crepe, Greek Fetish Omelets, Chickichanga, soups, salads, and much more!

Kobe's Japanese Steak House & Sushi Bar

8350 International Drive, Orlando, FL 32819;
407-352-1158

Japanese; C; $$–$$$; R; Dinner

If you are hungry and like Japanese, this is the place to visit. Diners can choose between eating in a group where the chef prepares your food in front of you with entertaining tricks and commentary or at the sushi bar. Portions are large and very filling, as you get several courses including salad (with a ginger sauce), soup, vegetables, fried rice, lo mein noodles, and your meat of choice. When I was in college, this was the restaurant of choice whenever we had a birthday to celebrate.

Roy's Restaurant

7760 West Sand Lake Road, Orlando, FL 32819;
407-352-4844; www.royrestuarant.com

Hawaiian fusion; D; $$$; S; dinner only

Hawaiian-inspired cuisine by celebrity chef Roy Yamaguchi will make you long for the island life. Roy's menu features fresh local ingredients with European sauces and bold Asian spices, always with a focus on seafood. Be sure to try Roy's Signature Hawaiian Martini and Mai Tai, as well as the Maui Wowie Salad.

Ruth's Chris Steak House

7501 Sand Lake Road, Orlando, FL 32819; 407-226-3900
610 North Orlando Avenue, Winter Park, FL 32789;
407-622-2444
www.ruthchris.com

Steakhouse; D; $$$; S; dinner only

As one of our favorite steakhouses—my friends and I frequently visit this popular steak house for special occasions. My drink is the Caramel Apple Martini. For wine lovers, the list is endless. All of the food is delicious, but I am a steady fan of the New York strip. In addition to great food and drink, the service is always impeccable, and valet parking is complimentary.

Merideth, Heather, Erin, and me after a wonderful meal at Ruth's Chris Steak House for my 29th birthday.

Salt Island Restaurant

7500 International Drive, Orlando, FL 32819;
407-996-7258; www.sirestaurant.com

Fish market/chophouse; C; $$–$$$; S; dinner

You'll feel like you are in an underwater world at this deep-sea dining establishment. Offerings include every type of seafood you can imagine from oysters to prawns to swordfish to lobster, as well as land-lover favorites such as steaks, rotisserie chicken, and lamb. Local jazz artists play nightly in the Wave Bar, while Caribbean guitar is played for at the Sand Bar. The restaurant boasts more than 250 vintage wine selections and 40 martini choices. Be sure to try the Raspberry Mojito.

Samba Room

7468 West Sand Lake Road, Orlando, FL 32819;
407-226-0550; www.sambaroom.net

Latin; C; $$–$$$; S; lunch (Monday–Friday), dinner

Samba Room offers a lively, music-filled atmosphere along with your favorite Latin-inspired dishes. With an extensive wine list, excellent mojitos, 25 specialty rums, 25 tequilas, and a premium cigar list, the restaurant offers all you need to have a good time. Every Friday Samba Room hosts a Latin deejay and salsa lessons. On Saturdays, they have a live Latin band. We went on a Thursday for a friend's birthday and had a great time. We feasted on great calamari and paella.

Cara and Heather play the bongos at Samba Room.

Seasons 52

7700 Sand Lake Road, Orlando, FL 32836;
407-354-5212; www.seasons52.vom

American; C; $$; S; Lunch, dinner

At this fresh grill and wine bar, girlfriends will be shocked to discover that these delectable appetizers, entrées and desserts are low fat and low calorie. A casually sophisticated grill and wine bar allows you to discover the sensational flavors of a seasonally changing menu. The restaurant serves highly flavored meals that are healthy and focus on the best of each season.

Using natural cooking techniques gives the food a great taste with fewer calories than similar restaurant meals. To compliment the flavor and aroma of your meal, Seasons 52 offers an adventurous international wine list of more than 140 outstanding wines, with 70 available by the glass. Be sure to save room for dessert, which is served in a shot-sized glass.

Texas de Brazil

5259 International Dr. Suite F-1, Orlando, FL 32819;
407-355-0355; www.texasdebrazil.com

Brazilian steakhouse; C; $$$; S; lunch, dinner

An authentic Brazilian steakhouse (*churrascaria*) featuring seasoned grilled meats carved right at your table, a salad bar with more than 40 items, fresh-baked Brazilian cheese bread, sweet fried bananas, and the signature cocktail, the *caipirinha*. This is sure to be a dining experience unlike any other, as you control the amount of food served by *gauchoesque* servers hoisting swordlike skewers with your green and red cards.

The Melting Pot

7549 West Sand Lake Road, Orlando, FL 32819;
407-903-1100; www.meltingpot.com
From I-4, Exit 74A

Fondue; C; $–$$; S; dinner

Love fondue but never prepare it at home? Then be sure to stop by The Melting Pot to indulge in your favorite cheese and chocolate fondues, as well as special dipping sauces to accompany your meal. Specializing in four-course fondue, extensive wine service, and a fun specialty alcoholic and nonalcoholic drink menu, The Melting Pot, with its casual atmosphere, will surely delight any Girls Getaway group.

"A real friend will tell you when you have spinach stuck in your teeth."

Vines Grill & Wine Bar

Fountains Plaza Bay Hill
7563 West Sand Lake Road, Orlando, FL 32819;
407-351-1227; www.vinesgrille.com

One of Orlando's newest upscale restaurants and jazz lounges, located on "Restaurant Row," minutes from the convention center, Vines offers an excellent dining experience in an intimate Chicago-style environment. *Specializes in dry-aged USDA prime beef and fresh fish and seafood, cooked over live natural wood-charcoal.* Also features an extensive selection of fine wines from around the globe.

Universal

Emeril's

Universal City Walk, 6000 Universal Boulevard, Orlando, FL 32819; 407-224-2424; www.emerils.com

New Orleans cuisine; C; $$$$; S; lunch, dinner

The outrageous Emeril Lagasse is the chef-proprietor of nine restaurants, including Orlando's Emeril's, which is located in Universal CityWalk. Upon entering the restaurant, you will see the metal staircase, the Gertjejansen artwork, the Wall of Wine, the Ochsner portrait, and the Food Bar. Enjoy a classic New Orleans cocktail and the high-energy, bold, exciting flavors of your meal and have an unforgettable experience.

The Palm Restaurant

Hard Rock Hotel, 5800 Universal Boulevard, Orlando, FL 32819; 407-503-7256; www.thepalm.com

Steak and seafood; C; $$$; S; Lunch, dinner

When you step into The Palm, you are entering more than 75 years of fun and celebration that have been ongoing. You'll recognize this instantly by the famous caricatures on the walls signifying the celebrities and pop culture icons that frequent this establishment from coast to coast. In addition to the friendly, upbeat atmosphere, The Palm delivers outstanding American cuisine with exceptional service.

Winter Park

Beluga

460 North Orlando Avenue, Winter Park, FL 32789; 407-644-2962; www.beluga-restaurant.com

Seafood, Steakhouse; C; $$$–$$$$; R; dinner

A popular choice for an elegant yet casual and fun evening out with friends, Beluga features indoor dining as well as an outdoor, covered dining area. With signature martinis, unique appetizers (including caviar, Wagyu Beef Tartar, and homemade potato chips with roasted garlic/horseradish/blue cheese fondue) and amazing seafood and steak entrées, you are sure to have an incredible meal. Examples of Beluga's unique offerings include blackened jumbo shrimp with crayfish/parmesan grits, crab crusted grouper, and popcorn crusted halibut. To add to your dining experience, the restaurant features three bars, including a glass top piano bar with live nightly entertainment. A great drink at Beluga is the Prickly Pear Margarita. Valet parking is available.

Bosphorous Turkish Cuisine
108 South Park Avenue, Winter Park, FL 32789; 407-644-8609

Turkish; C; $$$; S; lunch, dinner; closed Mondays

Named after the Bosphorous Strait, which separates the European and Asian parts of Istanbul. You will easily be transported to the Mediterranean country without even leaving Park Avenue. Enjoy authentic Turkish, music, décor, and food. The dishes are unique, and as long as you are an adventurous diner, worth trying. A popular dish is the *hunkar begendi,* or Sultan's Delight, which is chunks of seasoned beef sautéed with onions and tomatoes complimented by a cream-based puree of smoked eggplant. Live music and belly dancing every other Thursday night.

Briarpatch Restaurant
252 North Park Avenue, Winter Park, FL 32789; 407-628-8651

Deli; C; $$; NR; breakfast, lunch, dinner

My favorite dining destination on Park Avenue and a restaurant we frequented during our college years, this quaint indoor/outdoor café cooks up delicious meals for breakfast, lunch, and dinner. No meal will disappoint, but be sure to save room for the delectable homemade ice cream or giant pieces of scrumptious cake, which you can view through a turntable glass case when you enter. During nice weather, be sure to snag a seat outside so you can view the park.

Brio Tuscan Grille

Winter Park Village, 480 North Orlando Avenue, Winter Park, FL 32789; 407-622-5611; www.brioitalian.com

Italian; C; $$$; S; brunch (Saturday and Sunday), lunch, dinner

Boasting Tuscan-style steaks, classic Italian entrées, and an in-house bakery, Brio offers its guests "La Dolce Vita" (the good life), which focuses on enjoying quality meals with family and friends. The villa-like interior features Italian-style décor. The lasagna is delicious! Outside seating is preferred on days with nice weather.

You'll find a second location at the Mall at Millenia, 4200 Conroy Road, Suite 154, Orlando, FL 32839; 407-351-8909.

Café De France

526 Park Avenue South, Winter Park, FL 32789; 407-647-1869; www.lecafedefrance.com

French; C; $$$; S; lunch (Tuesday–Saturday), dinner, closed Sunday and Monday

This charming and quaint restaurant café features excellent French cuisine food with indoor and outdoor sidewalk seating. You'll almost mistake Park Avenue for the streets of Paris once you feast on excellent French cuisine.

Chef Justin's Park Plaza Gardens

319 Park Avenue South, Winter Park, FL 32789; 407-645-2475; www.parkplazagardens.com

European/Floridian; C; $$$; NR: Brunch (Sunday), lunch, dinner

Join Chef Justin Plank (named one of Central Florida's "Top 20 Chefs" by Restaurant Forum) as he prepares some of the area's best seafood, salads, and desserts in a delectable setting on Park Avenue. Choose to dine alfresco, on Park Avenue, or in the quaint, European-esque garden courtyard. The menu changes frequently but always provides a great selection of innovative dishes that will not disappoint. This is truly a unique dining experience you are sure to enjoy.

Dexter's of Winter Park

558 West New England Avenue, #100, Winter Park, FL 32789; 407-629-1150; www.dexwine.com

American; C; $$; NR; lunch, dinner

Dexter's is a Winter Park original with more than twenty years in the area. A favorite post-college yuppie hang out, Dexter's offers a fun, lively atmosphere with excellent, fresh food that changes monthly. Also known for its wine selection, Dexter's offers more than thirty red and white wines, champagne, ports, and sherries by the glass. Live music with no cover, edgy artwork, and an urban feel gives this ultra-hip restaurant and wine bar super cool status. Dexter's is a must-visit location for our college reunion trips to Orlando.

Another Dexter's is located in downtown Orlando in the Thornton Park area at 808 East Washington Street, Orlando, FL 32801. For more information, call 407-648-2777.

Sharon showing off her favorite restaurant in Orlando—Dexter's.
She has been a huge fan since we were in college.

Fleming's Prime Steakhouse & Wine Bar

933 North Orlando Avenue, Winter Park, FL 32789;
407-699-9463; www.flemingssteakhouse.com

Steakhouse; D; $$–$$$$; S; dinner only

Stylish, contemporary dining is the hallmark of Fleming's. The menu features the finest in prime beef, augmented by a tempting variety of chops, seafood, chicken, fresh salads, generous side orders (I recommend the creamed spinach), and indulgent desserts. The celebrated wine list, known as the Fleming's 100, boasts some of the finest wines in the world, all available by the glass.

Luma On Park

290 South Park Avenue, Winter Park, FL 32789; 407-599-4111; www.lumaonpark.com

Contemporary American; C; $$–$$$; dinner daily, brunch Saturday–Sunday

One of Winter Park's newest and trendiest restaurants, Luma offers an array of contemporary cuisine and fine wines. Be sure to try the tasty and attractive Southern Blossom Martini. Stop in for a quick light bite or stay for an entire meal. A great place to people-watch.

P. F. Changs China Bistro

Winter Park Village, 436 North Orlando Avenue, Winter Park, FL 32789; 407-622-0188; www.pfchangs.com

Chinese; C; $–$$; NR; lunch, dinner

Fresh, contemporary, consistent quality is what makes P. F. Changs a popular dining destination. Offering a combination of modern Chinese cuisine, excellent service, a great wine and specialty drink list, and tempting desserts all served in a stylish bistro. Working in a dramatic exhibition kitchen, chefs use Mandarin-style wok cooking to prepare the dynamic menu. My favorites include the chicken lettuce wraps, the lemon chicken, and the sweet-and-sour chicken.

A second location is at the Mall of Millenia, 4200 Conroy Road, # A144, Orlando, FL 32839; 407-345-2888.

Tolla's Italian Deli Café

240 North Pennsylvania Avenue, Winter Park, FL 32789;
407-628-0068; www.tollatolla.com

Italian; C; $–$$; NR; lunch, dinner

A tiny but very good Italian restaurant located a few blocks west of Park Avenue, Tolla's offers the very best in Italian food from pizza to chicken parmesan to brushetta. A favorite is the Stuffed Chicken Tolla, chicken breast stuffed with spinach, prosciutto, and feta over linguini with marinara sauce. Beer and wine served with live music every night from Thursday to Saturday.

Wazzabi Sushi & Japanese Steakhouse

1408 Gay Road, Winter Park, FL 32789;
407-647-8744; www.wazzabisushi.com

Sushi, Japanese; C; $$; NR; Lunch, dinner

Locally owned and operated, Wazzabi is located across from the Winter Park Village and offers diners a hip, modern indoor and outdoor atmosphere with delicious food. My favorite is the appropriately named Heaven Roll, which features coconut shrimp, avocado, scallion, and asparagus wrapped with tempura Kani and smothered with a mix of Japanese mayo, lime zest, chili oil, scallions, and five spices. A key feature that separates this from other Asian restaurants is the homemade cooking sauces prepared by Chef Soukanh "Cool" Vongkhamsene… delicious! The restaurant also features a fun martini menu and a good wine list.

CHAPTER 6

Where to Get Pampered

N o Girls Getaway weekend would be complete without some serious pampering. Luckily for you, Orlando features spas galore, ensuring the only stress you will encounter is deciding which spa to visit. You and your girlfriends can enjoy massages, body treatments and wraps, pedicures, manicures, facials,

Spa day with Leigh and Liz.

waxes, haircuts and color, and more. Many spas also offer a gym, whirlpool or Jacuzzi, showers with massaging jets, a sauna and/or steam room, and a relaxation or meditation room. Purchase a package of treatments and spend a leisurely morning or afternoon taking advantage of all of the amenities your spa has to offer.

Disney/Lake Buena Vista

Canyon Ranch SpaClub at Gaylord Palms Resort

Gaylord Palms Resort
6000 West Osceola Parkway, Kissimmee, FL 34746;
407-586-4772; www.canyonranch.com

Hours: Monday–Friday 9 A.M.–9 P.M., Saturday–Sunday 8 A.M.–9 P.M.

Find true relaxation in this 20,000-square foot, full-service spa, which features services such as body treatments, facials, massages, exotic Ayurveda treatments, fitness training, nutrition consulting, salon services, and makeup application. A basic 50-minute massage is $115, with an 18 percent gratuity automatically added.

Disney's Grand Floridian Resort & Spa

4401 Grand Floridian Way, Lake Buena Vista, FL 32830-1000;
407-824-2332; www.disney.ca/vacations/disneyworld/II/B/11/spa

Vacationers will find private treatment rooms, a couples' treatment room, and lounges. Separate men's and women's locker rooms include sauna, whirlpool, and steam room. Full-day, half-day, and individual treatments are available for facial therapy, massage, water therapy and soaks, body therapy, spa to go, hand and body treatments, and health and fitness services. A 50-minute Swedish massage costs $110.

Downtown

Eō Inn & Urban Spa

227 North Eola Drive, Orlando, FL 32801;
407-481-8485; www.eoinn.com

Located in the heart of downtown and on Lake Eola, this quaint yet modern boutique urban spa offers facials, massages, manicures, pedicures, body care, and waxing, with a personal touch. A 50-minute Swedish massage is $70.

Renovatio—A Medical Spa

Thornton Park, 4 North Summerlin Avenue, Orlando, FL 32801;
407-835-1911; www.feelofaspa.com

Hours: Tuesday–Friday 10 A.M.–7 P.M., Saturday 10 A.M.–5 P.M., Sunday 10 A.M.–5 P.M., Monday by appointment only

Renovatio offers one of the most advanced skincare and rejuvenation centers in Orlando. Guests are treated with the latest technology and receive expert consultations from a skilled professional staff that is overseen by a board-certified plastic surgeon. Renovatio offers FDA-approved procedures such as Botox, laser hair removal, IPL-skin rejuvenation, cellulite acne and wrinkle reduction, microdermabrasion, weight loss/detoxification, and SpectraMed Spa System. A 50-minute Swedish massage costs $75.

The Spa of Thornton Park

23 North Summerlin Avenue, Orlando, FL 32801;
407-649-8889; www.spaorlando.com

Hours: Monday–Thursday 10 A.M.–6 P.M., Friday and Saturday 9 A.M.–8 P.M.; Sunday 10 A.M.–5 P.M., Sunday

Centrally located in downtown Orlando, near the corner of Summerlin and Washington. You cannot miss the yellow house with a red door. The spa offers a wide assortment of massages, facials, body treatments, skin care, and nail care. A great way to enjoy the spa with friends is to book a spa party with 5 to 12 of your friends. The cost is $100 per person, and your group will enjoy two 30-minute spa treatments, appetizers, and wine. A basic 50-minute massage is $70. This is one of my favorite spas!

Leigh's spa party at The Spa of Thornton Park.

International

Shala Salon & Day Spa

Two locations:
The Peabody Hotel, 9801 International Drive;
Orlando, FL 32819; 407-248-8009
Plaza Venezia, 7726 West Sand Lake Road;
Orlando, FL 32819; 407-248-8828
www.shalasalon.com

Hours are Monday–Saturday 9 A.M.–8 P.M. and Sunday, 10 A.M. –6 P.M.

Shala Salon & Day Spa services include haircuts, coloring, manicures and pedicures, skin care, massage services, hair and eyelash extensions, and makeup. Additional services include a unique microderm facial to reduce wrinkles and scars, remove fine lines, and get healthier looking skin, as well as endermologie and body wrap treatments designed to reduce cellulite. A Swedish massage starts at $80. All major credit cards are accepted.

The Ritz-Carlton Spa

4012 Central Florida Parkway, Orlando, FL 32837;
407-393-4200; www.ritzcarlton.com

Although it was ranked as the top U.S. spa by *Travel & Leisure* magazine, some friends report it is quite pricey. The 40,000-square-foot spa features 40 treatment rooms, a 4,000-square-foot outdoor heated lap pool and healing waters, co-ed relaxation conservatory, full-service Carita salon, tranquility/spa boutique, and a 6,000-square-foot Wellness Center. Signature treatments include: Tuscan citrus cure, Thai massage, East Indian lime scalp and body massage, Ashiatsu, and Ionithermie cellulite and toning program. A 50-minute Swedish massage costs $110.

Universal

Mandara Spa at Portofino Bay Hotel at Universal Orlando

5601 Universal Boulevard, Orlando, FL 32819;
407-503-1244; www.universalorlando.com

Hours: Daily 7 A.M.–10 P.M.

The Mandara Spa is a sanctuary where you can relax and discover the elixir of youth—not as a goal but as a moment of blissful reverie. Enjoy therapies such as the traditional javanese lulur, the elemis visible brilliance facial, miracle micro therapy, cellutox and ocean wraps, ionithermie cellulite reduction, and gentle touch tooth whitening. Mandara Spa offers customized and personalized treatments to fit any need. Spa packages are available, or guests may opt to utilize the spa on an à la carte basis. The experience will be one of pampering, total relaxation, and calm.

Winter Park

Euro Day Spa & Salon

800 Formosa Avenue, Winter Park, FL 32789;
407-740-0444; www.euro-day-spa-salon-orlando.com

Hours: Monday–Friday, 9 A.M.–6:30 P.M.;
Saturday, 8:30 A.M.–6:30 P.M.; Sunday, 10 A.M.–5 P.M.

Euro Day Spa combines a collection of spa therapies for relaxation, stress reduction, pain relief, and beauty. Decorated with colorful European art, the spa provides treatments for massage, spa, skin, hair, nails, toning/cellulite, pain management, and much more! A basic 45-minute massage is $70.

The Beauty Spot

364 West Fairbanks Avenue, Winter Park, FL 32789;
407-772-4500; www.beautyspotinc.com

Hours: Monday 10–7, Tuesday–Thursday 9–8,
Friday–Saturday 9–9, Sunday 11–7

Skin therapies, massages, body treatments, spa packages, waxing, makeup application, and hair extensions are all services offered at this Winter Park favorite. My friend Darcy says it is a fun place to get a manicure/pedicure—and be sure to ask for Michael.

CHAPTER 7

Where to Find Culture and Entertainment

I n a region where theme parks dominate, girlfriends may be surprised to find a diverse cultural landscape of museums, galleries, and performing arts in the Orlando area.

Museums

Albin Polasek Museum and Sculpture Gardens

633 Osceola Avenue, Winter Park, FL 32789;
407-647-6294; www.polasek.org

Listed on the National Register of Historic Places and showcasing nearly 200 of Czech Republic-born Albin Polasek's works in his home, galleries, and 3-acre garden. In addition to Polasek's work, the museum also features rotating exhibits by other leading artists and touring collections.

Gallery and gardens open September 1–June 30, Tuesday–Saturday 10–4, Sunday 1–4 P.M. Admission is $5 for adults, $4 for seniors, and $3 for students.

Cornell Fine Arts Museum at Rollins College

1000 Holt Avenue, Winter Park, FL 32789;
407-646-2526; www.rollins.edu/cfam/

Rollins College's newly renovated Cornell Fine Arts Museum is considered one of America's top college art museums and home to Florida's oldest and one of its most distinguished collections. The once-nondescript building nestled on the shores of Lake Virginia has been transformed into a spacious architectural jewel that doubles its gallery space and shows off its panoramic lake view.

Gallery hours are Tuesday–Saturday 10 A.M.–5 P.M. and Sunday 1 A.M.–5 P.M. Admission is $5 for adults. There is no charge for CFAM Members or Rollins College faculty, staff, and all students with current IDs.

Charles Hosmer Morse Museum of American Art

445 North Park Avenue, Winter Park, FL 32789;
407-645-5311; www.morsemuseum.org

The museum is home to the world's most comprehensive collection of works by glass artist Louis Comfort Tiffany, as well as exhibits of pottery and 19th- and 20th-century paintings. The variety of the Morse's Tiffany holdings range from his famed leaded-glass windows to glass buttons he fashioned to make even life's most humble objects expressions of beauty available to a broad public. It includes paintings and extensive examples of his pottery, as well as jewelry, enamels, mosaics, watercolors, lamps, furniture, and scores of examples of his Favrile blown glass. Of particular interest is the Morse's extensive American

Art Pottery collection, which now numbers more than 800 examples of the richly creative 19th-century American Art Pottery movement.

Museum hours are Tuesday, Wednesday, Thursday, and Saturday 9:30–4; Friday 9:30–8 P.M. September–May, 9:30–4 June–August; Sunday: 1–4. Closed Monday and major holidays except for Easter and July 4. Admission is $3 for adults and $1 for students.

Mennello Museum of American Art
900 East Princeton Street, Orlando, FL 32803;
407-246-4278; www.mennellomuseum.org

From I-4, take the Princeton exit

Owned and operated by the City of Orlando, the Mennello is Florida's only museum showcasing works of self-taught artists, including renowned folk artist Earl Cunningham. Folk art was a prime product of the new American democracy, which strongly represented the spirit of this country. American folk art is the art of the people—often forgotten men and women. But American folk art is not an unskilled imitation of fine art. It is produced by amateurs who work for their own gratification and the applause of their families and neighbors, and by artisans and craftsmen of varying degrees of skills and artistic sensitivity who work for pay.

Museum hours are Tuesday–Saturday 10:30 A.M.–4:30 P.M.; Sunday noon–4:30 P.M. Closed Mondays and major holidays. Admission is $4 for adults, $3 for seniors (60-plus), and $1 for student with valid ID; museum members always admitted free.

Orange County Regional History Center

65 East Central Boulevard, Orlando, FL 32801;
407-836-8500; www.thehistorycenter.org

With five floors of Florida's past, exhibits display the history of central Florida, ranging from Florida's native inhabitants to European voyagers to the beginnings of Disney World. If you want a historical recap of this area, be sure to visit the Center's permanent exhibits, which are complemented by special exhibits on display throughout the year. Traveling exhibits are also on display featuring Florida artists and Florida historical overviews.

Hours: Monday–Saturday 10 A.M.–5 P.M., Sunday noon–5 P.M. Admission: $3.50–$7

Orlando Museum of Art

2416 North Mills Avenue, Orlando, FL 32803;
407-896-4231; www.omart.org

Located in Loch Haven Park in downtown Orlando, OMA's purpose is to enrich the cultural life of Florida by providing excellence in the visual arts. Founded in 1924, OMA presents 10–12 exhibitions onsite each year, as well as art enrichment programs, gallery tours, and art appreciation lectures. From 6–9 P.M. on the first Thursday of each month, OMA's atmosphere changes with themed exhibitions by local artists, live music by popular local bands or deejays, a cash bar, and refreshments.

Hours: Tuesday–Friday 10 A.M.–4 P.M., Saturday–Sunday noon–4 P.M. Admission: $5–$8

Orlando Science Center

777 East Princeton Street, Orlando, FL 32803;
407-514-2000; www.osc.org

The Orlando Science Center strives to provide science for everyone by creating opportunities for experiential science learning and promoting science literacy. The Center caters to adult groups. Call for more details. In addition, every third Friday night, the Center features a Cocktails & the Cosmos event featuring food, live entertainment, and cocktails for $9.95.

Hours: Monday–Thursday 9 A.M.–5 P.M., Friday and Saturday 9 A.M.–9 P.M., Sunday 1–5 P.M. Adult admission: $8.95–$14.95

Galleries

Grand Bohemian Gallery

The Westin Grand Bohemian Hotel
325 South Orange Avenue, Orlando, FL 32801;
407-581-4801; www.grandbohemiangallery.com

The mission of the gallery is to enhance environments with inspiring art for today's collector by featuring artwork from national and international artists specializing in contemporary painting, art glass, ceramics, jewelry, and sculpture. The gallery's services include art consulting, corporate gift programs, wedding registry, framing, authentication, restoration, and preservation.

Hours: Monday 9:30 A.M.–5:30 P.M., Tuesday–Saturday 9:30 A.M.–10 P.M., Sunday 10 A.M.–3 P.M.

Millenia Fine Art Gallery

555 Lake Destiny Drive, Orlando, FL 32801;
407-266-8701; www.milleniaarts.com

Featuring paintings by Picasso, Chagall, Renoir, and other masters as well as works by contemporary artists in a distinctive Bauhaus architectural setting. An array of media from modern masters to contemporary international artists is exhibited, satiating the appetite of the most discerning art connoisseur, as well as the humble novice.

Hours: Tuesday–Thursday 10 A.M.–6 P.M., Friday–Saturday 10 A.M.–7 P.M. Admission: Free

Timothy's Gallery

236 Park Avenue, Winter Park, FL 32789;
407-629-0707; www.timothysgallery.com

A contemporary craft gallery, Timothy's has been named one of the "Top 100 Gallery of American Craft" winners since 1997. The gallery features artistic jewelry of precious metals and stones; custom designs; raku; blown, fused, slumped glass; woven throws; gifts and wedding registry; silk or woven jackets and scarves; ceramics; jewelry boxes; journals; lamps; whimsical doodads; artful home and personal accessories; wedding and commitment bands; and metal sculpture.

Monday–Saturday 10:00 A.M.–5:30 P.M.; Sunday 1:00 P.M.–5:00 P.M.

Performing Arts

Bob Carr Performing Arts Centre

4603 West Colonial Drive, Orlando, FL 32801;
407-849-2020 (box office); www.orlandocentroplex.com

Located downtown across from the TD Waterhouse Arena, this theater/concert hall features continental style seating for 2,500. Ideal for concerts, Broadway presentations, the symphony, ballet, and opera, it features excellent acoustics and sound capabilities. The Centre hosts excellent plays and performing arts series during the year.

Cirque du Soleil—La Nouba

Downtown Disney; 1478 East Buena Vista Drive, Orlando, FL 32830; 407-939-7600; www.cirquedusoleil.com

Featuring surreal sets, live music, and high-energy choreography with gymnasts, acrobats, dancers, and clowns, Cirque du Soleil's permanent show La Nouba is featured at Downtown Disney. Performances are held Tuesday–Saturday at 6 P.M. and 9 P.M. There are no performances on Sundays and Mondays.

Orlando Philharmonic Orchestra

812 East Rollins Street, Suite 300, Orlando, FL 32803;
box office: 407-770-0071; www.OrlandoPhil.org

The Orlando Philharmonic Orchestra is Central Florida's resident orchestra, appearing in more than 105 performances each season. As a fully professional ensemble, the Orlando Philharmonic engages the talents of more than 80 professional musicians from around the globe. The Philharmonic's mission is to foster and promote symphonic music through excellence in performance, education, and cultural leadership.

Gardens

Harry P. Leu Gardens

1920 North Forest Avenue, Orlando, FL 32803;
407-246-2620; www.leugardens.org

These gardens feature miles of paved scenic walkways that take you through garden settings. Here, you can see America's largest Camellia collection outside California and the largest formal rose garden in Florida, a house museum dating from the 1880s, palm and bamboo garden, the new Tropical Stream Garden and Kitchen Garden with herbs, vegetables, and a butterfly garden! Open daily from 9–5 except Christmas day. Leu House Museum tours from 10 A.M.–3:30 P.M. every 30 minutes. The Leu House Museum is closed for repairs and inventory in July.

Hours: Daily from 9 A.M.–5 P.M., except Christmas Day. Admission: $5 for adults; free each Monday from 9 A.M.–noon

Sports and Concerts

Disney's House of Blues

Downtown Disney
1490 East Buena Vista Drive, Lake Buena Vista, FL 32830;
407-934-BLUE; www.hob.com

Decorated in quintessential New Orleans style, the HOB is best known for its live music. The Orlando HOB hosts musical acts from all genres, so be sure to visit its website for acts performing during your trip.

Disney's Wide World of Sports Complex

Walt Disney World, Lake Buena Vista, FL 32830;
407-363-6262; disneyworldsports.disney.go.com

This 220-acre state-of-the-art facility is the ultimate destination for athletes, fans, and sports lovers. With more than 170 amateur and professional events each year, this complex provides a place where athletes can compete and experience the same world-class facilities. If you are a sports enthusiast, visit the complex's website for more information and upcoming events.

Florida Citrus Bowl Stadium

1610 West Church Street, Orlando, FL 32805;
407-423-2476; www.fcsports.com

This 70,000-seat facility is home to the annual Florida Citrus Bowl and the University of Central Florida Knights football. For baseball fans, the 5,500-seat Tinker Field adjoins the stadium. Both facilities are part of the Orlando Centroplex.

Hard Rock Live Orlando

Universal Studios CityWalk
6050 Universal Boulevard, Orlando, FL 32819;
407-351-LIVE; www.hardrock.com

A 3,000-capacity concert venue located at Universal Studios CityWalk showcases music from national acts to emerging artists. Hard Rock Live and the 600-seat Hard Rock Cafe Orlando, also a great venue for live music, are situated in a 140,000-square-foot building designed as a retro interpretation of the Roman Coliseum.

TD Waterhouse Centre

4603 West Colonial Drive, Orlando, FL 32801;
407-849-2020 (box office); www.orlandocentroplex.com

The TD Waterhouse Centre serves as home to the Orlando Magic of the NBA, Orlando Predators, and various world-class sporting and entertainment events. One of my girlfriends and I worked at the Orlando Magic games in college, so an NBA game is a must when we return. Be sure to check the events schedule when planning your weekend. You never know when your favorite performer may be in town.

Enjoying an Orlando Magic game.

CHAPTER 8

Where to Find Nightlife

Orlando is host to a popular and thriving nightlife, no matter what part of town you are visiting. Options range from dinner clubs to entertainment complexes to live entertainment to pubs to wine bars to dance clubs. No matter what you are in the mood for, Orlando will make sure you and your girlfriends have a great night.

> *"There are shortcuts to happiness, and dancing is one of them."*
> —VICKI BAUM

Disney/Lake Buena Vista

Pleasure Island

Downtown Disney Marketplace
1780 Buena Vista Drive, Lake Buena Vista, FL 32830;
407-824-2222; www.downtowndisney.com

It is always New Year's Eve at Pleasure Island, with fireworks, live dancers, and confetti every night. At Downtown Disney's

Pleasure Island, enjoy seven clubs for one admission price of $23. Clubs range from 8 Trax, a seventies and eighties dance club, to Mannequins Dance Palace to Adventures Club and the Comedy Warehouse, both comedy clubs, to Rock 'N' Roll Beach Club. The BET Soundstage offers the latest in R&B and the Wildhorse Saloon offers country music complete with line dancing. There is no admission charge before 7 P.M.

House of Blues

Downtown Disney Marketplace
1490 East Buena Vista Drive, Lake Buena Vista, FL 32830;
407-943-BLUE; www.hob.com

With a true blues vibe, the Orlando HOB provides great entertainment in a 1,500-capacity venue. Be sure to check the schedule as acts range from world-famous performers to up-and-coming talent in genres ranging from rock 'n' roll, gospel, R&B, Latin, reggae, hip-hop and, of course, the blues. Tables are limited, so if you want a seat, be sure to arrive early. Food is available.

Downtown Orlando

Bösendorfer Lounge

Westin Grand Bohemian
325 South Orange Avenue, Orlando, FL 32801; 407-313-9000

Boasting a casual, hip atmosphere where guests can relax in luxury, the Bösendorfer features live classical and contemporary jazz music. Although drinks can be pricey, the lounge was voted the "Best Place to Sip Martinis" by the Orlando *Business Journal* and voted Best Hotel Bar by *Orlando Weekly*. Worth the visit alone are the original works of art featured throughout.

Sharon and me toasting our chocolate martinis at the Bösendorfer Lounge after the Magic game.

Casey's On Central

50 East Central Boulevard, Orlando, FL 32801; 407-648-4218

Although a hurricane altered my 30th birthday Key West trip, my girlfriends made it up to me with a visit to Casey's On Central, completely decorated in a Key West motif. This quaint bar is a favorite local hangout with a huge outdoor patio, great music, and stiff drinks.

Erin and Heather helping me celebrate my
30th birthday at Casey's On Central.

Cowboy's Orlando

1108 South Orange Blossom Trail, Orlando, FL 32805;
407-422-7115; www.cowboysorlando.com

Cowboy's Orlando is Orlando's premier country bar. Open Thursday–Saturday nights 8–2 A.M. with Ladies Night every Thursday and free line dance lessons each evening. Everyone 18 and up is welcome. We went here after the Keith Urban concert on a Thursday night and had fun but felt "older" than the rest of the crowd. The other nights may be different.

Club Paris

122 West Church Street, Orlando, FL 32801;
407-981-7500; www.clubparis.net
(Main entrance on Garland between South and Church streets.)

Decorated in custom-made Italian furnishings, Club Paris is a decadent and state-of-the-art party spot. Co-owned by the popular heiress Paris Hilton, who is even known to make cameo appearances. Guests can enjoy one of many dance areas, hydrate at multiple bar stations and lounge areas, or experience the exclusive second-level VIP area, where private dance floors and a relaxing bedroom-like experience await. Special nightly features include Latino Night on Wednesday and Ladies Night on Thursday.

Eola Wine Company

500 East Central Boulevard, Orlando, FL 32801; 407-481-9100; www.eolawinecompany.com

Located on the corner of Orange Avenue and Central, this popular and trendy wine bar features the comforts of a small café with 70 wines by the glass, 11 wine flights, 30 microbrewed beers, tapas, appetizers, and desserts. Created as a place where friends can visit, share stories, and laugh, Eola Wine Company is a great place to visit with the girlfriends.

Be sure to visit its second location in Winter Park at 1236 South Park Avenue.

Room 3 Nine

39 North Orange Avenue, Orlando, FL 32801; 407-841-0390; www.room3nine.com

A laid-back, vintage atompshere comprised mostly of downtown folk enjoy the jazz vibe at this place. An extensive wine and martini list, along with several domestic and international beer and microbrew selections are available. Appetizers and snacks are also available. Happy hour is Monday–Friday, 4–8, and features two-for-one drafts and $3 well drinks. Three-for-one specials on Friday until 7.

SKY60

64 North Orange Avenue, Orlando, FL 32801; 407-246-1599

This rooftop bar offers excellent views of downtown Orlando while the young professional crowd takes to the dance floor. The stylish, cabana-inspired bar offers fun cocktails such as the mojito and pepperita. Guests can sit on white beach furniture while they take in the scenery. Ladies Night is typically held each Tuesday.

Tanqueray's

100 South Orange Avenue, Orlando, FL 32801; 407-649-8540

The bar/restaurant is located below street level in what used to be a bank vault but today serves as a popular power-lunch spot for Orlando's power elite. The locals rave about the bartenders' skill at pouring a Guinness pint as well as the Tanqueray martinis. On Fridays and Saturdays, there is excellent live jazz and blues. No cover.

Wall Street Plaza

Wall Street Plaza, with eight colorful bars and restaurants lining a brick-paved street, is a great starting point for an evening of club hopping in the heart of historic downtown.

Located off Orange Avenue, Wall Street features a multitude of bars, each with a different vibe. Here you can find whatever type of nightlife you crave. From **Wall Street Cantina,** a relaxed outdoor Mexican bar and restaurant, to **One-Eyed Jacks,** a dance place with an oversized bar and a stage, to **The Globe,** a relaxed coffee shop offering unique appetizers and authentic sushi and a 4–7 P.M. weekday happy hour, to **Waitiki Retro Tiki Lounge**, offering island-style beverages and live music, to **Monkey Bar,** a trendy martini bar with outdoor lounge chairs and a bird's-eye view of Wall Street Plaza.

With Carly and Nikki at One-Eyed Jack's on Wall Street.

Wally's-Mills Avenue Liquors, Inc.

1001 North Mills Avenue, Orlando, FL 32803; 407-896-6975

Wally's has been the local "dive" bar for more than 50 years. Offering a "biker bar" feel and serving very strong drinks, Wally's is a must visit for girls wanting the dive bar experience and maybe a few strong, cheap drinks to get the night started. Despite its dingy feel, it also has some charm and coziness only found in establishments of this character. In addition, you never know if you might find the "who's who" of Orlando congregating here listening to the old jukebox. Parking is limited, so you may want to cab it. Open 8 A.M.–1 A.M. daily.

Ybor's Martini Bar

41 West Church Street, Orlando, FL 32801; 407-316-8006

Known by the locals for its apple martini, Ybor's offers a huge variety of hip, classy beverages including single-malt scotches, cognacs, and brandies. Named after the area in Tampa where the cigar factories are located, brave girlfriends can enjoy a cigar with their drink or participate in the monthly "cigar tasting." Ybor's often features live music and art showings.

International Drive

GLO Lounge Orlando

8967 International Drive, Orlando, FL 32819; 407-351-0361; www.gloloungeorlando.com

Located two blocks north of the Convention Center, GLO Lounge offers "glowing" ambiance in an upscale and hip hotspot. Dancing, billiards, and plasma TV provide entertainment for guests. No cover before 11 P.M.

Howl at the Moon

8815 International Drive, Orlando, FL 32819; 407-354-5999; www.howlatthemoon.com

Howl at the Moon is a total entertainment experience where the piano players and staff entertain the guests who inevitably become part of the show. The customers tend to be a diverse group comprised of guests of all ages. The regular clientele of Howl at the Moon is enhanced by traveling business people and conventioneers. Howl at the Moon is a hot spot for birthdays, anniversaries, and other celebrations.

Pointe*Orlando

9101 International Drive, Orlando, FL 32819;
407-248-2838

Located on I-Drive across from the convention center, Pointe* Orlando offers a mix of restaurants, clubs, shops, and movie theatres for both day and nighttime fun. B.B. King's Blues Club opens in 2007, offering fantastic Southern cooking and live music nightly. **The Grape**, an upscale wine bar, and **Taverna Opa**, featuring Greek food, music, and belly dancing, opened in winter 2006.

Winter Park

Austin Coffee and Film

929 West Fairbanks Avenue, Winter Park, FL 32789;
407-975-3364

A trendy, local hangout featuring organic coffee, tea, and beer in a low-key bohemian setting. The coffeehouse offers a wide array of activities throughout the week. Live music and comedians perform on the weekends, poets and writers are featured on Sundays, live painting takes place on Wednesdays, and Tuesdays and Thursdays are open mike nights. In addition, film nights, "Flicks on Fairbanks," are being planned.

Hours: Monday–Thursday 8 A.M.–11 P.M., Friday–Saturday 8 A.M.–1 A.M., Sunday 10 A.M.–midnight

Fiddler's Green Irish Pub & Eatery

544 W. Fairbanks Avenue, Winter Park, FL 32789;
407-645-2050; www.fiddlersgreenorlando.com

A quaint pub with a great beer selection, a fine wine list, traditional Irish food, and live music. This local favorite is open for lunch and dinner and features a weekday happy hour from 4–7 P.M.

Socca Ultra Lounge

Orange Avenue, Winter Park, FL 32789;
407-628-2333; www.popolobistro.com/socca

This funky neighborhood bar invites you in with its warm Moroccan/South Beach décor complete with cozy cushions. Girlfriends will enjoy the Chick Flick Cocktail, Liquid Tiramisu Martini, Chocolate Strawberry Tini, or the Dirty Blu Martini complete with a bleu cheese stuffed olive. Beer, wine, mixed drinks, appetizers, pizzas, and snacks are also available. Hours: Monday–Tuesday, 5 P.M.–midnight; Wednesday–Saturday, 5 P.M.–2 A.M.

Tatame Lounge

223 West Fairbanks Avenue, Winter Park, FL 32789;
407-628-2408; www.tatamelounge.com

This "Hong Kong-inspired lounge" presents a mix of music, art, tea, and sake in a bohemian-chic inspired atmosphere. Rice wine, fruit-infused sake, bubble tea, and light Asian fare are all unique draws to this very unique lounge. Deejays and live acts perform frequently. Tatame is open until 3 A.M. on the weekends.

Universal

Blue Martini

4200 Conroy Road, Orlando, FL 32839;
407-447-2583; www.bluemartinilounge.com

With nightly live music and more than 25 tasty martinis, the Blue Martini is a hip bar located at the Mall at Millenia. Listen or dance to the best in live entertainment while enjoying the tapas-style food menu. Unique martini choices include Almond Joy, Sex in the City, Banana Split, and Cantaloupe. Trendy attire is recommended after 6 P.M.

Hours: Monday–Friday 4 P.M.–2 A.M.; Saturday–Sunday 1 P.M.–2 A.M.

Universal CityWalk Orlando

1000 Universal Studios Plaza, Orlando, FL 32803;
407-363-8000; www.universalorlando.com

It's a 30-acre entertainment complex where you can experience the best of the best in live music, casual and fine dining, dancing, shopping, movies, and more. Experience five nightclubs and bars as well as seven restaurants: Hard Rock Café, Motown Café, Bob Marley—A Tribute to Freedom, Pat O'Brien's, Jimmy Buffet's Margaritaville Café, Latin Quarter, Red Coconut Club, the Groove, and City Jazz/Bonkerz Comedy Club, NBA

> *"Tell me, what is it you plan to do with your one wild and precious life?"*
> —MARY OLIVER

City, NASCAR Café. CityWalk has no charge for entrance, but individual venue cover charges apply. You can buy the CityWalk Party Pass with all club access for $13.95 (plus tax) or you can also add a movie and get the CityWalk Party Pass and Movie for only $13 (plus tax). CityWalk Operating Hours are daily from 11 A.M.–2 A.M.

Bachlorette party at Universal CityWalk.

Velvet Bar

Hard Rock Hotel
5800 Universal Boulevard, Orlando, FL 32819

A swank, upscale bar perfect for drinks and mingling, Velvet is a great hotel hangout. If you stay at a Universal Orlando Resort, ask the concierge about Velvet Sessions, an invitation-only rock 'n' roll cocktail party held the last Thursday of each month at Velvet Bar. Each "session" features a different beverage theme, along with great food and live entertainment from top names in the music industry.

Live Entertainment

Cirque du Soleil—La Nouba

Downtown Disney
1478 E. Buena Vista Drive, Lake Buena Vista, FL 32830;
407-939-7600; www.cirquedusoleil.com

Billed as a "theatrical ride for the senses," this is one of a handful of permanent Cirque du Soleil (French for "circus of the sun") displays around the world. Consistent rave reviews make this show, written and directed by Franco Dragone, a must-see for the whole family while in Orlando. The theater is set up so everyone has the best possible view. Then you have the performances, which feature unbelievably magical talent. Reservations can be made up to six months in advance.

Dolly Parton's Dixie Stampede

8251 Vineland Avenue, Orlando, FL 32821;
407-238-4455; www.dixiestampede.com

Girlfriends' icon Dolly Parton brings a taste of the wild west to Orlando. The action-packed dinner show extravaganza includes entertainment for everyone. Here you can watch amazing stunning performers, amazing horse feats, fantastic stunt riders, magic, as well as audience participation with a delicious four-course dinner extravaganza for less than $50 per person.

Improv Comedy Club & Restaurant

129 West Church Street, Orlando, FL 32801;
321-281-8000; www.orlandoimprov.com

Located in the historic Church Street Station of downtown Orlando (in the old Rosie O'Grady's building), the Improv is a perfect place for tons of laughs with your girlfriends. Dinner and show options also available. Contact the Improv for a schedule.

Medieval Times Dinner & Tournament

4510 West Irlo Bronson Memorial H, Kissimmee, FL 34746;
407-396-1518; www. medievaltimes.com

Set in a castle, this real-life action drama brings fantasy to life with a story that incorporates live horses, sword fights, knights in shining armor, and of course, romance. Guests dine on a feast of ribs, chicken, soup, potatoes, and beer per the medieval rules of etiquette (i.e., no utensils).

SAK Comedy Lab

380 West Amelia Avenue, Orlando, FL 32801-1101;
407-648-0001; www.sak.com

This comedy club is one of Orlando's most popular entertainment venues, featuring a variety of well-known comedians. Different themes are featured nightly, including the popular "Duel of Fools" (Thursday–Saturday) and Saturday's "Request Live." For those wanting to learn more about the trade, workshops are offered on Mondays; call for details. Casual attire is suggested, as are reservations.

Sleuths Mystery Dinner Show

8267 International Drive, Orlando, FL 32819;
407-363-1985; www.sleuths.com

This mystery show is performed in a dinner party atmosphere that serves as the backdrop for an undisclosed murder. Intriguing, mysterious, and funny plots will keep you on the edge of your seat as you participate by questioning suspects. The meal includes salad, appetizers, beer, and wine, and diners may choose lasagna, game hens, or prime rib for their main course.

CHAPTER 9

Where to Find Sports, Recreation, and Outdoor Activities

S hopping and spas tend to be girlfriend favorites, but many
people enjoy outdoor sports and other recreational activities
while visiting Orlando. For those interested in these activities, I
compiled a few typical options, from boating to horseback riding
to tennis and golfing. In addition, there are some nontraditional
options, such as ice skating, hot air balloon rides, and swimming with the manatees.

Belly Dancing

Suspira's Orlando Bellydance

421 West Fairbanks Avenue, Winter Park, FL 32789; 407-579-9765

Belly dancing is a fun way to exercise and spend time with your
girlfriends. At Suspira's, you can take one class for $12 or five
classes for $50, payable in advance via credit card. If you have
never tried it before, now is your chance!

Bicycle Rental

West Orange Trail—Bikes and Blades

17914 State Road 438, Winter Garden, FL 34787;
407-877-0600

Boating

Adventures in Florida

2912 East Marks Street, Orlando, FL 32803;
407-924-3375; www.adventuresinflorida.com

Specializing in canoe and kayak expeditions, this eco-tour company offers day-long or shorter tours in the central Florida area. They also offer full moon paddles. Day-long canoe trips cost about $55–$75 per person; includes lunch.

Boggy Creek Airboat & Monster Buggy Nature Tours

2001 East Southport Road, Kissimmee, FL 34746;
407-344-9550; www.bcairboasts.com

In business since 1994, this company can show you the real Florida either by air boat or swamp buggy. Tour options include day, night, nature, or private. There are two locations, so be sure to call for more information. Prices range from $20.95–$45 per person, plus tax.

Hours: 9 A.M.–5:30 P.M. everyday, including holidays

Winter Park Scenic Boat Tour

312 East Morse Boulevard, Winter Park, FL 32789;
407-644-4056; www.scenicboattours.com

This relaxing, narrated, one-hour cruise through 12 miles of beautiful lakes and canals of historic Winter Park has hosted many Winter Park visitors since 1938. Aboard the 18-passenger pontoon boat, you will see Rollins College, Kraft Azalea Gardens, Isle of Sicily, tropical birds, plants, flowers, and magnificent mansions. Hours are 10 A.M.–4 P.M. daily (except Christmas). Tours depart on the hour. Price is $10 for adults. Cash and checks only.

Bowling

All shopped-out on a rainy day and want to find some fun? Don't forget how much fun bowling can be. There are several bowling alleys in the Orlando area. For more information and game coupons, visit www.bowlorlando.com or www.florida bowling.com.

World Bowling Center

7540 Canada Avenue, Orlando 32819; 407-352-2695

Located in the I-Drive district, this basic 32-lane bowling alley features funky décor not standard at most bowling alleys. Prices for adults are $3.75 per game, except on Sundays when the adult price is only $2.50 per game. Shoe rental is $2.

Hours: noon–11 P.M. daily

Cooking

Chef Voila!

1140 Town Park Avenue, Lake Mary, FL 32746;
407-333-3262; www.chefvoila.com

Offering cooking classes, parties, a café, and retail shop, Chef Voila features classes on a variety of topics including Southern, Tasty Tailgates, Cooking with Wine, Gourmet Pizzas, and much more. Bring your aprons and favorite wine. The calendar changes frequently and prices vary, so visit the website or call for more details.

Truffles and Trifles

711 West Smith Street, Orlando, FL 32804;
407-648-0838; www.trufflesandtrifles.com

With more than twenty years in business, Truffles and Trifles is the largest, most successful cooking school in the southeast and was recently named one of the top five cooking schools in the country by the Food Network. A very fun learning experience that you will still be able to enjoy once you return home. Classes range from Mexican Fiesta to All Chocolate to Holiday Themes, with prices for basic classes from $45–$50. Also available are gourmet culinary delights in the shop and gift baskets for any fine food lover.

Hours: Monday–Friday 10 A.M.–5 P.M., Saturday 10:30 A.M.–3 P.M.

Farmers Markets

Sunday EolaMarket

Every Sunday starting at 9 A.M., join various local vendors for baked goods, fresh produce and flowers, beautiful plants and homemade crafts. The market is held on beautiful Lake Eola in downtown Orlando.

Winter Park Farmers Market

200 West New England Avenue, Winter Park, FL 32789
Hours: Open-air market; Saturday 7 A.M.–1 P.M., year-round

Fishing

Both fresh- and saltwater fishing in Florida can be a lot of fun. Orlando provides guide services to help make your fishing trip relaxing, fun, and hopefully successful. For any and all fishing in Florida, be sure to purchase a fishing license ($13.50–$31.50) by calling 888-347-4356. Lunch is not included, so you will either have to bring your own or plan to eat at a restaurant on the water. Most offer four-, six-, or eight-hour fishing trips, as well as transportation.

Champion Bass

Location depends on fishing trip;
407-738-7652; www.championbass.com

Offering bass, flats, and fly-fishing, Champion is one of the top fresh and saltwater fishing guides in the area. Rates start at $250 for two people. There is a $100 nonrefundable deposit when you book your trip.

Freelancer Guide Service

3096 Stillwater Drive, Kissimmee, FL 34743;
407-348-8764; www.orlandobass.com

In business since 1970, Freelancer is the oldest continuously operated bass guide service in central Florida. All Freelancer bass guides are full-time licensed professionals.

Rates start at $225 for two people for freshwater and $350 for two people for saltwater, plus any bait costs.

Golfing

With 168 golf courses and 18 nationally ranked golf academies, golf enthusiasts are sure to find the perfect course or school in the Orlando area. In fact, choosing your ideal course can be somewhat overwhelming. With that in mind, I recommend contacting Tee Times USA at 888-465-3356 or www.teetimesusa.com. This free service will help you select the best course for you, make reservations, and send driving directions to your hotel. Of course, several of the resorts mentioned in chapter 3 of this book feature great courses and golf schools as well.

For girls not quite ready to tackle an entire course, there are several miniature golf parks in the area. Most are located on I-Drive or near Disney.

Horseback Riding

For girls wanting to go horseback riding, there are a few places to ride near town. Trail rides or English or western riding lessons are available. Be sure to call for reservations.

Grand Cypress Equestrian Center

1 Equestrian Drive, Orlando, FL 32836;
407-239-1938; grandcypress.com/equestrian_center

Offering both English ($100) and western lessons ($45), the Center is located on State Road 535, Exit 68 off I-4.
   Hours: Weekdays 8:30 A.M.–6 P.M.; weekends 8:30 A.M.–5 P.M.

Horse World Riding Stables

3705 South Poinciana Boulevard, Kissimmee, FL 34758;
407-847-4343; www.horseworldstables.com

A working 750-acre ranch offering western trail rides for all riding levels. Prices range from $39–$69 plus tax per person. The stables are about 12 miles south of Highway 192. Hours: Daily 9 A.M.– 5 P.M.

Hot Air Balloons

Want a great way to start your day? How about a sunrise hot air balloon ride with a champagne brunch over Orlando? Although not cheap (typically $150–$200 per person for a 45- to 60-minute flight), it is a great way to see the city and have some fun in the air. Most balloon companies take credit cards and prefer morning flights.

Bob's Balloon Charters

732 Ensenada Drive, Orlando, FL 32825;
877-824-4606; www.bobsballoons.com

Bob's can fit four to six people per balloon. The company also offers hotel pickup service.

Blue Water Balloons

P.O. Box 560572, Orlando, Fl 32856;
800-586-1884; www.bluewaterballoons.com

Free hotel pickup available in the Orlando area. Limited to four passengers per balloon.

Pottery Painting

Glaze Under Fire

K-Mart Shopping Center (next to Michael's)
501 North Orlando Avenue, Suite 141, Winter Park, FL 32789;
407-644-8088; www. glazeunderfire.com

A great way to visit with friends and express your artistic abilities, pottery painting is also a great stress reliever. Studio fees range from $6–$9 per person, and you must also purchase your pottery. You are welcome to bring your own food and drink, including beer and wine, or order food from one of the nearby restaurants. This shop will have your piece ready for pickup in two weeks from the time you paint.

Hours: Monday 5–10 P.M., Tuesday–Thursday 11 A.M.–10 P.M., Friday and Saturday 11 A.M.–11 P.M., Sunday noon–6 P.M.

Studio 6 Pottery Studio

7541A Sand Lake Road, Orlando, FL 32819;
407-903-7278; www.mystudio6.com

Near Universal and International Drive, this paint-your-own pottery shop will have your piece ready in three or four days from the time you paint. Studio fees are about $8 per person.

Hours: Monday–Saturday 1 A.M.–10 P.M., Sunday noon–8 P.M.

Skating

RDV Sportsplex

8701 Maitland Summit Boulevard, Orlando, FL 32810;
407-916-2550; www.rdvsportsplex.com

Located off I-4 on exit 90, the RDV offers public ice skating daily beginning at noon on weekdays. The concession stand is open during all public skating sessions. Evening, weekend, and afternoon times vary, so call for details. Ice skating fees are from $5.50–$7.52 plus tax. Ice skate rental fees are $1.88 plus tax. Schedule and rates are subject to change.

Swimming/Scuba

Fun 2 Dive Scuba and Manatee Tours

503 South French Avenue, Sanford, FL 32771;
888-588-DIVE; www.fun2dive.com

Located outside Orlando, Fun 2 Dive offers daily manatee tours, manatee snorkeling trips, scuba charters, scuba classes, and snorkeling. Cost for a manatee tour is $85 per person for a full day, including snacks and gear with six people maximum. Transportation not provided.

YMCA Aquatic and Family Center of Orlando

8422 International Drive, Orlando, FL 32819;
407-363-1911; www.ymcaaquaticcenter.com

For those who enjoy swimming indoors, the YMCA offers three heated pools with lanes for swimming laps, as well as a diving well. Located on I-Drive, nonresidents are charged $10 per day.

Hours: Monday–Friday 6 A.M.–9 P.M., Saturday 8 A.M.–5 P.M., and Sunday noon–4 P.M.

Tennis

Orlando Tennis Centre

649 West Livingston Street, Orlando, FL 32801;
407-246-2161; www.cityoforlando.net

Fees for singles are $5.02 (1½ hours, soft court), doubles are $5.02 (two hours, soft court), singles are $4.02 (1½ hours, hard court), doubles are $4.02 (2 hours, hard court).

Hours: Monday–Friday 8 A.M.–9:30 P.M., Saturday and Sunday 8 A.M.–2:30 P.M.; closed: Thanksgiving, Christmas Day, and New Year's Day

Water Sports

Buena Vista Watersports

13245 Lake Bryan Drive, Lake Buena Vista, FL 32830;
407-239-6939; www.bvwatersports.com

This privately owned recreational watersports facility is located on Lake Bryan, a secluded, natural spring-fed lake with white sandy beaches, and lush tropical foliage surrounded by cypress trees. Activities include Jet Ski rentals ($50–$90) and boat charters ($70–$130).

Orlando Watersports Complex

8615 Florida Rock Road, Orlando, FL 32824;
407-251-3100; www.orlandowatersports.com

A unique watersports park designed for wakeboarding, wakeskating, and waterskiing, the complex is perfect for those wanting to learn water sports to advanced water enthusiasts. Also featured on site are a mini motor cross and a paintball course. Hours and prices vary depending on desired sport and level of experience. A snack bar is onsite.

Wine Tasting/Making

Global Grapes

127 West Church Street, Suite 106, Orlando, FL 32801;
407-849-5066

This quaint family-owned-and-operated wine shop in downtown Orlando provides helpful staff that will assist you in finding the perfect wine. The shop offers free delivery within a 1-mile radius of the store, themed wine tastings each Wednesday, happy hour, custom gift baskets, and buy-one-get-one free specials at select times. The entrance is on Pine.

Grapes to Glass

501 North Orlando Avenue #325, Winter Park, FL 32789;
407-331-9463; www.grapestoglasswp.com

Winter Park Shopping Center (Corner of Lee Road and Webster Street)

Host your own wine-tasting or wine-making party. Wine tastings usually involve groups of ten to twenty, last from one-and-a-half to two hours and include a paring of fruits, cheeses, crackers, and chocolates if requested. Prices range from $15–$25 per person. Wine making involves two nights: wine making the first evening, then bottling, corking, and customizing your bottles the second evening. Guests will leave with about four or five bottles per person, and costs are about $65 per person for both evenings. Call for more information or to book your wine-tasting or -making event.

The Wine Room

270 Park Avenue South, Winter Park, FL 32789;
407-696-9463; www.thewineroomonline.com

The only establishment in central Florida to offer the Enomatic wine-serving system, which allows wine enthusiasts to sample more than 150 wines at the touch of a button with the technology to preserve the taste and quality. With a warm, inviting, and relaxing setting, The Wine Room also features rare selections of cheese, meats, pates, and appetizers to complement your wine-tasting experience.

Yoga and Pilates

College Park Yoga

706 West Smith Street, Orlando, FL 32804; 407-999-7871

Although I have not personally attended this studio, it is highly recommended as a premier yoga studio, balancing the physical and mental benefits of yoga and focusing on both an energizing, strength-building workout as well as a restorative mental cleanse. Attentive to both beginners and advanced, this locally-owned-and-operated studio is run by a couple deeply committed to this discipline.

Full Circle Yoga

972B Orange Avenue, Winter Park, FL 32789; 407-644-3288; www.fullcircleyoga.com

Yoga classes are offered every day of the week and serve beginners through advanced students, including special classes for pregnant women and new mothers. Basic and intermediate hatha yoga and a full complement of Ashtanga yoga classes are taught. Classes are ongoing; you may start anytime. Just show up. If it is your first class, plan to arrive 10 to 15 minutes early. A single class is $13. Please visit the website or call for a schedule.

Pilates Loft

1909 N Orange Avenue, Orlando, FL 32804; 407-898-4641

With great instructors, call to see how they can best accommodate your group's needs.

CHAPTER 10

Where to Go for Side Trips

If you want to stay in the Orlando area, but also want to experience some favorite girlfriends side trips, be sure to check out these nearby hot spots.

Cocoa Beach

Although Orlando is located in the middle of the state, you can easily get to the beach within an hour drive. A favorite nearby beach is Cocoa Beach,

> *"As we travel across the life span, we make friends and friends make us."*
>
> —LETTY COTTIN POGREBIN, WRITER

which is just south of Kennedy Space Center and Cape Canaveral. The Space Coast also offers some great surfing, clean beaches, and the world-famous Ron Jon Surf Shop (www.ronjons.com). Ron Jon also houses Craig Carroll's Cocoa Beach Surfing School (321-868-1980), where you can learn how to surf and also rent surfboards, skim boards, wetsuits, kayaks, beach bikes, and other gear. Cocoa Beach (www.ci.cocoa-beach.fl.us) is also a great place to watch a shuttle launch.

Daytona USA

1801 West International Speedway Boulevard,
Daytona Beach, FL 32114;
386-947-6800; www.daytonausa.com

For NASCAR fans or girls who like life in the fast lane, a side trip to Daytona USA will prove to be a great experience. Located approximately one hour north (east) of Orlando, at Exit 129 off I-4, Daytona USA is a 60,000-square-foot interactive motor sports attraction. Activities include: Speed Channel's "You Call the Race," where guests play TV announcer and "call" a major Daytona race finish; EA Sports "NASCAR Thunder" allows participants to use computer technology to drive a stock car on the high banks of Daytona; and Heroes of the Track, an opportunity to question one of your favorite NASCAR drivers using DVD technology. The most popular is the Richard Petty Driving Experience (1-800-BEPETTY), where guests can ride along or even drive a NASCAR-style stock car on the Daytona International Speedway.

Kennedy Space Center

SR 405, Kennedy Space Center, FL 32889; 321-449-4444;
www.kennedyspacecenter.com

Just 45 minutes from Orlando is NASA's launch headquarters—the only place on Earth where you can tour launch areas, meet an astronaut, see giant rockets, train in spaceflight simulators, and even view a launch. The complex boasts a full-service, sit-down restaurant as well as numerous self-service restaurants and specialty food locations. Maximum access admission is $38 plus tax for adults and includes the KSC tour and all visitor complex exhibits, shows, and movies and admission to the Astronaut Hall of Fame. Parking is free.

Hours: Daily 9:30 A.M.–5 P.M.

Mount Dora

A favorite for antique shopping, Mount Dora is approximately 25 miles northwest of Orlando. This quaint city has the nostalgic feeling of a small town, complete with large canopy oak trees, historic buildings, rolling hills, and gorgeous lakes. Mount Dora was recognized by the readers of *Florida Living* magazine as Florida's friendliest small town and as having the best antique shopping area in the state. For more information and for upcoming events and festivals, call the Mount Dora Area Chamber of Commerce at 352-383-2165; or visit www.mountdora.com.

Lakeridge Winery & Vineyards

19239 U.S. 27 North, Clermont, FL 34717;
800-768-WINE; www.lakeridgewinery.com

Located in nearby Clermont, visiting a winery and vineyard also makes for a fun girlfriends excursion. Here, you and the girls can take a tour, have a picnic, and sample wines from Florida's largest vineyard. Lakeridge is a 127-acre estate in gently rolling countryside about 25 miles west of downtown Orlando. Complimentary tours and wine tastings held seven days a week; Monday–Saturday 10 A.M.–5 P.M., Sunday, 11A.M.–5 P.M.

Call in advance for group tour rates, as well as upcoming arts and crafts festivals, jazz concerts, and grape stomping.

Wekiwa Springs State Park

1800 Wekiwa Circle, Apopka, FL 32712;
407-884-2008; www.floridastateparks.org/wekiwasprings

Located about 20 minutes north of Orlando at exit 94 off I-4, this 7,000-acre state park centers around the Wekiwa River, one of Florida's only federally and state designated scenic and wild rivers. Activities include bicycling, hiking, snorkeling, swimming, canoeing, camping, picnicking, fishing, and wildlife viewing. Amenities include several camping areas, a nature center, two picnic pavillions, access to Wekiwa Springs, Wekiwa Springs Run, Rock Springs Run, and the Wekiva River, and horse, hiking, and boardwalk nature trails.The park is open from 8 A.M. till sundown year round. The nature center is open Saturday and Sunday from noon– 3 P.M. Park admission fees are $5 per car for two to eight people.

West Orange Trail

501 Crown Point Cross Road, Winter Garden, FL 34787;
407-654-5144; www.dep.state.fl.us

Just a few miles from downtown Orlando and Walt Disney World, the 19-mile West Orange Trail is a rail-trail, which travels through the communities of Winter Garden and Apopka. Among the highlights along the trail are a xeriscaped butterfly garden about a mile east of the Oakland Outpost, the Winter Garden Historical Museum, and some picturesque views of Lake Apopka. The trail also provides access to and from Clarcona Horseman's Park, offering equestrians a staging area for their visits. The constant changes in scenery and the relaxed atmosphere of the towns along the way make this a great ride. This trail will eventually be a part of the 200-mile planned regional connection known as the Central Florida Loop.

CHAPTER 11

Annual Area Happenings

W ith so much to do in Orlando, you may want to schedule your getaway trip around an annual area happening. From garden shows to art festivals, from sporting events to musical events, there are spectacular goings-on in Orlando all year round. This chapter highlights some of the more exciting you may wish to attend. For more Orlando events, please visit www.GirlsGetawayGuide.net.

January

Disney World Marathon
Held the beginning of each year, the event features the 26.2-mile marathon, as well as a half-marathon and other distances. For information, email wdw.sports@disney.com or visit disneyworldsports.disney.go.com.

February

Mount Dora Art Festival
About three hundred artists from across the state and the country exhibit their works of glass, metal, ceramics, watercolors,

photography, sculpture, jewelry, and much more here. With strict selection standards ensuring quality art, more than 200,000 visitors attend this well-known festival held annually since 1975. You can also watch street performers entertain and free concerts at the various Mount Dora parks. For information, call 352-383-0880; or visit www.mountdoracenterforthehearts.org.

Winter with the Writers Festival

The oldest continually running literary festival in the state, bringing the finest contemporary writers of our time to Central Florida. The festival, which is sponsored by Rollins College, brings world-renowned authors and poets to Winter Park every Thursday in February for book signings, seminars, and readings. For information, visit www.rollins.edu.

February–March

Atlanta Braves Spring Training

Experience the fun of spring training in Florida as the Atlanta Braves compete in the Grapefruit League against other National League teams. Games are held at the Cracker Jack Stadium at Disney's Wide World of Sports Complex in Lake Buena Vista. Tickets range from $13–$21 and can be purchased by calling 407-839-3900; or visit atlanta.braves.mlb.com.

Winter Park Bach Festival

This annual festival hosts a variety of orchestral and choral performances paying tribute to classical composers such as Bach, Mozart, and Schumann. For information, visit www.bachfestival florida.org.

February–April

Mardi Gras at Universal Studios

This spectacular celebration in Universal Studios Florida is held each Saturday night in the spring. Enjoy live music and spectacular parades with floats from New Orleans! For information, visit www.universalstudios.com.

March

Central Florida Home & Garden Show

Homeowners can find millions of decorating ideas, building and remodeling solutions, and landscaping tips at the all-new, expanded Central Florida Home & Garden Show at the Orange County Convention Center's new North Building on International Drive. For information, call 800-645-7798; or visit www.orlandohomeshow.com.

Winter Park Sidewalk Art Festival

Held each year, this festival features the work of numerous artists who specialize in clay, painting, drawing, jewelry, photography, glass, and much more. Drawing more than 350,000 spectators each year, the festival also offers outdoor entertainment and refreshments. For information, visit www.wpsaf.org.

April–June

Epcot International Flower and Garden Festival

From breathtaking flowers to whimsical topiaries, your senses will come alive as you take in the cornucopia of colors and scintillating scents of these spectacular blossoms. View the extraordinary garden displays representing the international themes of Epcot's World Showcase Disney's style. For information, call 407-824-2222; or visit www.wdwinfo.com.

May

Florida Music Festival

Held mid-May, the FMF features more than 250 artists, 200 music industry execs, and 20,000 music fans who gather at several downtown Orlando venues to celebrate up-and-coming bands and artists. For information, visit www.floridamusicfestival.com.

Orlando International Fringe Festival

Fringe is a festival or celebration of the theatrical and performing arts. The 10-day Orlando International Fringe Theatre Festival takes place in and around downtown Orlando. Frequently referred to as "the premier springtime cultural event in Central Florida," the festival features more than 500 "uncensored" and "nonjuried" shows. For information, call 407-648-0077; or visit www.orlandofringe.org.

June

WineQuest Wine Tasting & Auction

Central Florida's premier wine event, outside Walt Disney World, is a 10-day celebration of wine tastings, dinners, auctions, and seminars. Designed to educate and entertain guests, the main goal is to raise funds to support Quest, Inc., an organization dedicated to improving the lives of people with disabilities. For tickets and information, call 407-889-4530; or visit www.winequest.org.

June–August

Sounds of Summer

Featuring musicians from the Philharmonic performing at the Harry P. Leu Gardens. For information, call 407-896-6700.

July

Independence Day Celebrations

Orlando loves to celebrate the Fourth of July. With fireworks held at Disney World, Universal Studios, and downtown at Lake Eola, girlfriends are sure to find a great location to celebrate this historic day.

September

ABC Super Soap Weekend

Held at Disney MGM each year, this soap opera convention hosts some popular daytime stars as attendees are treated to an inter-active weekend with their favorite actors and actresses from the

ABC daytime dramas *All My Children, One Life to Live, General Hospital*, and *Port Charles*. ABC Super Soap Weekend is the largest soap fan event held anywhere in the country. Festivities include autograph sessions, motorcades, interviews and talk shows, game shows, musical performances, and the chance to purchase one-of-a-kind memorabilia from the shows. Admission to the ABC Super Soap Weekend is included in the regular theme park admission to Disney-MGM Studios. For future updates and more information, call the Super Soap Hotline at 407-397-6808; or visit abc.go.com/daytime/supersoap/wdw/index.html.

September–May

Orlando Ballet

Orlando Ballet is central Florida's only fully professional Ballet Company. The 33-year-old organization performs through its annual season spanning eight months at the Bob Carr Performing Arts Centre. For information, visit www.orlandoballet.org.

September–November

International Food & Wine Festival

If you love great food, wine, and live music, this is one festival you should attend. Held at Epcot each year, more than twenty food marketplaces with food and wine from around the world are featured, as well as your favorite celebrity chefs and hosts from the Food Network. In typical Disney fashion, entertainment is first class with a live "Eat to the Beat" concert series and performers from Cirque Du Solieil's La Nouba. Appetizer-sized portions of the international traditional cuisine range from $1.50–$4.50. During the festival, more than 1,200 beer and wine tastings are scheduled with complimentary samples. Your Epcot admission is all you need to attend the festival. For information, visit wdwinfo.com.

October

Halloween Horror Nights

Held each year at Universal Studios, this event is Orlando's—and quite possibly the world's—largest, most terrifying Halloween celebration. Halloween Horror Nights is a special ticket event and is $59.75 plus tax for day of event. Florida residents can purchase discounted tickets in advance. For more information or to purchase tickets, visit the website, the front gate of the theme parks, or Florida Spencer's gift locations. Because of the event's popularity, tickets for weekend nights should be purchased far in advance. For information, visit www.halloweenhorrornights.com.

October–June

NBA's Orlando Magic

The key sporting events at downtown's TD Waterhouse Centre, the Orlando Magic games are always a good time. The Orlando Magic joined the NBA for the 1989–1990 season. The franchise had only a brief period of adjustment before establishing itself as a contender and one of the league's most popular teams. For ticket information, call 407-89-MAGIC; or visit www.nba.com/magic.

November

Downtown Disney Annual Festival of the Masters

More than 200 honorees from art festivals around the country will showcase painting, photography, glass works, sculpture, printmaking, drawing, jewelry, and for the first time, digital art. Live entertainment and children's activities also will be a part of the weekend-long event. For information, visit www.wdwinfo.com.

International Food and Wine Festival

Travel around Epcot World Showcase Lagoon and sample the exquisite variety of cuisines of more than 25 international marketplaces representing more than 30 countries and regions. For information, call 407-824-4321; or visit www.wdwinfo.com.

December

Disney Magical Holidays

Each year, Disney celebrates the holiday season with festive parades, light shows, concerts, and snow on Main Street. For information, visit www.wdwinfo.com.

ICE! (www.gaylordpalms.com/ice)

If you thought you wouldn't see ice in Orlando, think again. Each year the Gaylord Palms Resort presents the hand-carved holiday attraction from nearly 2 million pounds of ice that creates a winter experience like no other in Florida. For more information and exact dates, call 407-586-4423.

CHAPTER 12

Personal Favorites

Several people ask me what my favorite this or that is, so I've compiled a list in this chapter. Of course, this may change, but as of printing these are my current faves in each category:

Favorite Hotel: Westin Grand Bohemian (Downtown)

Favorite Outdoor Shopping: Park Avenue/Winter Park

Favorite Mall: Mall at Millenia

Favorite Outlet: Orlando Premium Outlets

Favorite Gallery: Millenia Fine Art Gallery

Favorite Museum: Cornell Fine Arts Museum

Favorite Martini Spot: Blue Martini

Favorite Breakfast: The Briarpatch

Favorite Lunch: Chef Justin's Park Plaza Gardens

Favorite Dinner: HUE Restaurant

Favorite Fun Dinner: Café Tu Tu Tango

Favorite Sushi: Wazzabi Sushi & Japanese Steakhouse

Favorite Live Music: House of Blues

Favorite Live Entertainment: Cirque du Soleil

Favorite Entertainment Complex: Universal City Walk

Favorite Theater: Bob Carr Performing Arts Centre

Favorite Side Trip: Mt. Dora Antiquing

Favorite Sunday Brunch: House of Blues Gospel Brunch

Favorite Steak Restaurant: Kres Chophouse & Lounge

Favorite Wine Bar/Restaurant: Dexter's

Favorite Festival: Winter Park Art Festival

Favorite Sporting Event: Orlando Magic games

Favorite Recreation Activity: Belly Dancing

Favorite Spa: The Spa at Thornton Park

Favorite Clothing Boutique: Zou Zou Boutique

---

*For new and exciting hot spots
plus more favorites, please visit*

www.GirlsGetawayGuide.net

CHAPTER 13

Helpful Sources to Plan Your Trip

No matter how you arrive in Orlando, navigating your way around the city is easy. Orlando's public transit system is not very tourist-friendly, so I'd recommend renting a vehicle if you plan to do a fair amount of traveling within the city. If you don't have your own vehicle, taxis are a convenient way to get to your destinations. Additionally, pedicabs are a fun way to get around downtown and the I-Drive areas. Visitors to the I-Drive area can hop aboard the I-Drive trolley. Several hotels offer a shuttle service, so be sure to inquire when making your reservations. For more information about planning your Girls Getaway to the Orlando area, please visit www.GirlsGetawayGuide.net.

Airport Shuttle

Beeline Ground Transportation (407-438-3969)

Mears (407-423-5566)

Taxis

Ace Metro/Luxury Cab (407-855-1111)

Diamond Cab Company (407-523-3333)

Star Taxi (407-857-9999)

Town & Country Transport (407-828-3035)

Yellow/City Cab (407-699-9999)

Pedicabs

Orlando Pedicab (321-217-2233)

Why Walk Pedicab (407-740-8294)

I-Ride Trolley Service

(www.iridetrolley.com)

With 11.5 million trips logged since it started service in 1997, the I-Ride Trolley Service has provided travel to many of the 20 million annual visitors to International Drive Area.

Emergency numbers

Orlando Police Department
100 South Hughey Avenue, Orlando, FL 32801; 407-246-2470

Orange County Sheriff's Department
2500 West Colonial Drive, Orlando, FL 32804; 407-254-7000

Hospitals

Florida Hospital-Orlando

601 East Rollins Street, Orlando, FL 32803; 407-303-6611

Orlando Regional Medical Center

1414 Kuhl Avenue # Mp41, Orlando, FL 32806; 407-841-5111

For additional information and local happenings:

Orlando/Orange County Convention & Visitors Bureau, Inc.

6700 Forum Drive, Suite 100, Orlando 32821; 407-363-5800; www.orlandoinfo.org

Orlando Regional Chamber of Commerce

75 South Ivanhoe Boulevard, Orlando, FL 32804; 407-425-1234; www.orlando.org

Orlando *Sentinel*

633 North Orange Avenue, Orlando, FL 32801; 407-420-5000; www.orlandosentinel.com

Be sure to visit the *Sentinel*'s "Calendar" section each Friday for an updated list of local happenings.

INDEX

Give the Gift of

Girls Getaway Guide to Orlando

Leave Your Baggage at Home

to Your Friends and Colleagues

CHECK YOUR LEADING BOOKSTORE OR ORDER HERE

❏ YES, I want _____ copies of *Girls Getaway Guide to Orlando* at $13.95 each, plus $4.95 shipping per book (Florida residents please add 98¢ sales tax per book). Canadian orders must be accompanied by a postal money order in US funds. Allow 15 days for delivery.

My check or money order for $_____ is enclosed.

Please charge my: ❏ Visa   ❏ MasterCard
                     ❏ Discover ❏ American Express

Name _____

Organization _____

Address _____

City/State/Zip _____

Phone_____ Email _____

Card # _____

Exp. Date_____ Signature _____

Please make your check payable and return to:
Gray Dog Publishing
P.O. Box 2589, Orlando, FL 32802
Order online at www.GirlsGetawayGuide.net